FLIPPER'S SIDE

Paul Hodgson

This book is dedicated to the memory of my mother
Alice (1930-1994)

The names of certain people mentioned in this book
have been changed in the interests of privacy.

ISBN 0-9538791-0-0

 First published in the United Kingdom in 2000 by Paul Hodgson.

Produced for the author by Scarsdale Books (Publishing Services) of Darlington.

ACKNOWLEDGEMENTS

The author would like to thank the following people:
First and foremost, Mike Jarvie who edited and wordprocessed my original audiotapes. This book, which went through many drafts, would not have been possible without his invaluable assistance and creative input.
I am also indebted to Jill Scott, Clare Scully and Eve Bussey for their constant support and the staff at Darlington Reference Library for their endless patience.

FOREWORD

Every football club throughout the land has a hard core of fans like Paul Hodgson, who follow their team both home and away, in all weathers, supporting them loyally through thick and thin (though in the case of Darlington FC mostly the latter). Paul also happens to be a veteran fund-raiser for various charitable causes and even became involved in the campaign to save the Quakers from extinction in 1982.

Yes indeed, every football club in all four divisions and non-league as well can lay claim to a small number of these dedicated supporters, but how many of them could manage to do all of the things I've mentioned above, and more, from a wheelchair?

I first met Paul back in 1979 when he was only fourteen years old. I had recently signed forms as a professional footballer for Darlington and was jogging around the pitch, recovering from an ankle injury. Paul and I got talking and as a result of that conversation we forged a lasting friendship.

Two things struck me on that particular day – one was the fact he was on his own, which meant that he must have got there under his own steam. And as anyone who has ever visited Darlington's Feethams ground will know, if you are coming from the town centre on foot you have to negotiate a busy ring road and also walk around the perimeter of the cricket pitch before you reach the East Stand paddock[1], which is where I encountered Paul, sitting in his wheelchair. He informed me that he had accomplished this hazardous journey entirely on his own. The second thing that struck me was his remarkable knowledge about all things connected with Darlington FC and football in general. As a result of that first meeting it was obvious to me that his mental faculties were as sharp as a tack.

Throughout my career there have been so many moments that still bring a smile to my face, and my early years at Darlington supplied a good percentage of them. There was the time when the manager's underpants went missing from his peg in the changing room and were later found hanging from his car aerial – I genuinely thought a marquee had been erected in the club car park! And then there was that old standby of the deep-heat treatment – a favourite amongst footballers. This involved spraying the shorts of our centre-forward, John Borthwick, with Ralgex, just before the start of a game. He never stopped running that day – if memory serves me

[1]The old wooden East Stand, dating back to 1919, was demolished in 1997 and replaced with a new cantilever structure, which was opened in readiness for the start of the 1998-99 football season. [Ed.]

right, I think he even scored a hat trick![2]

To be part of the schoolboy antics of a bunch of professional footballers is a unique experience. Luckily, Paul himself, given his long association with the club, not only witnessed his fair share of practical jokes but was also a leading player in the story that I'm now about to tell.

In 1982 the Supporters' Club invited a few of the players, including myself, to a 'gentlemen's evening,' an event that Paul helped to arrange. The players' seats were ominously situated in the front row, and I quickly sussed out that one of us was to be selected by the two strippers to get up on stage with them. So, as they made their entrance, I swiftly made my way to the back of the room, having learned that I was their intended victim.

In place of me, our centre-forward was dragged on stage, whereupon the two strippers produced the dreaded talcum powder, baby oil and tie. The rest of the proceedings I will leave to the reader's imagination, but the hilarious sights of that evening will be forever etched on my mind.

Word soon spread to the club itself about the goings on that night and so I, together with the star performer (our centre-forward) and one of our midfield generals, were all summoned to the manager's office. The gaffer at that time was Billy Elliott, a former Sunderland player and manager, who listened to our feeble excuses and then proceeded to rip us apart.

My alibi, however, was watertight. Plenty of witnesses had seen me at the back of the room. Our midfield general held one hand up; he had, after all, gathered up the victim's discarded clothes, because the two of them shared digs together, so he had to plead guilty as charged. The centre-forward, though, didn't have a leg to stand on and so he sensibly owned up – 'Fair cop, gaffer!'

When the verdict was announced an hour later we were all surprised to see Paul sitting sheepishly in the reception area outside the manager's office, like a naughty schoolboy waiting to be caned by the headmaster. He'd been summoned because of his part in organising the event, which was the source of much amusement. Once inside the gaffer's office I got away scot-free – phew! The midfield general was fined and the centre-forward was threatened with the sack, but because the manager knew we wouldn't score another goal all season if we released him, he was fined instead.

It then fell to Paul's turn to go in and incur the wrath of Billy Elliott. Needless to say, his face was the colour of the ghost in *Randall and Hopkirk (Deceased)*. While he was trying his best to cut a sorry and pathetic figure, I

[2]John Borthwick's only hat trick for the club was against Stafford Rangers in April 1990. Perhaps this is the game in question. [Ed.]

peeped through the gaffer's office window and began pulling stupid faces, at which Paul couldn't help smirking. I heard the boss blowing a fuse and screaming that it was no laughing matter. Paul's sentence was duly passed – he was banned from the ground for a week – and I scarpered before the transfer list was mentioned again.

To this day, Paul is still my memory bank, which I plug into when I want to recall past football events and devilment. Strangely enough, in our first meeting back in 1979, I made a statement to the effect that one day I would play in what was then the old First Division. This I eventually achieved, but only briefly, with Coventry City in 1987, which was the year we won the FA Cup against Tottenham. And who was it that reminded me of that prophecy years later? Yes, you've guessed it – Paul.

In 1989 after spells at Rotherham United, Coventry City and York City I rejoined Darlington under Brian Little, and I'm pleased to be able to say that I captained the side during one of the club's most successful periods, which meant not only gaining promotion from the GM Vauxhall Conference at the first attempt but also winning the Fourth Division title the following season. Just as satisfying, though, was the knowledge that Paul too was actively involved in the dramatic events of those two promotion campaigns, this loyal fan who not only supported me throughout my career but also those hundreds of other players, past and present, who have graced the black and white of Darlington FC.

Kevan Smith
(Hull City Assistant Manager)

Chapter 1

When I was just a little boy,
I asked my mamma, 'What should I be?
Should I be Darlo?
Should I be Poolie?'[1]
Here's what she said to me:

'Wash your mouth my son,
Go get your father's gun,
And shoot the Poolie scum,
Shoot the Poolie scum.'

(To the tune of 'Que Sera Sera')

As the reader will soon come to understand, I'm a big fan of Darlington Football Club (otherwise known as Darlo and nicknamed the Quakers.) The thirty box files of match-day programmes and fanzines, all neatly labelled and piled up in a wardrobe of my spare bedroom, bear eloquent testimony to my enduring obsession. At a rough guess, I must have nearly two thousand programmes from most of the Quakers' home and away matches in league and cup, dating back to the 1960s. Perhaps in years to come, long after my ashes have been scattered on the pitch, you'll see some expert in football memorabilia assessing my valuable collection on the *Antiques Roadshow!*

Out of the current ninety-two English Premier and Football League grounds I've now been to seventy-eight, though not, I hasten to add, all with Darlo. I've been to over forty non-league grounds as well and have even been known to attend the occasional reserve game and pre-season friendly. Like the author of *Fever Pitch*, I'm a bit of a trainspotter when it comes to my love of football. I've been following the Quakers for over a quarter of a century. Their struggles to avoid relegation became mine and those even rarer moments of success were savoured to the full.

My support for the club has never wavered and it has even furnished me with an apt nickname. Allow me to explain. During one away game, now regrettably lost in the abyss of time, we scored, and in attempting to clap I missed! On the spur of the moment one of the fans behind me conceived an

[1] i.e. a supporter of Hartlepool United Football Club.

appropriate name to commemorate this feat of cackhandedness, a name that stuck – *Flipper.*

The non-disabled reader might be wondering why it is that I feel so passionately about something in which I'll never take part. That would, however, be an inaccurate assumption, since I did play in goal for my school football team until I was sixteen and also represented the school at various disabled sporting events. In any case, how many fans standing on the terraces with their beer guts bulging from their trousers, could have ever seriously contemplated playing football at the professional level? Very few, I suppose. And why is it that football grounds have disabled areas in the first place? For the simple reason that disabled supporters get as much pleasure from supporting their team or seeing a goal being scored as any able-bodied fan.

As one of my early heroes, the Darlington centre-forward, John Stalker, once said to me, for that split-second when the ball hits the back of the net the sensation he felt coursing through his body was even better than reaching an orgasm. And I could well understand where he was coming from, if you'll forgive the pun! For my part, I always experience that same rush of adrenalin when a Darlington player scores a goal.

What follows is therefore an account that seeks to chart the steady progress of the football virus through my bloodstream and how it radically changed the course of my life for the better. First, I must speak of an earlier, potentially disastrous viral infection that almost cut short my life before it had even begun.

When I was only seven months old I was taken ill with flu-like symptoms. Our family doctor reassured my mother, telling her not to worry. But when I suffered an epileptic fit a few days later and a second doctor was called out I was immediately admitted to hospital. Incredibly, a further two days went by until the hospital confirmed that I had contracted meningitis. By then the disease had affected my brain and spinal cord. Because of the delay in diagnosing my condition, the consultant told my mother to prepare for the worst. Fortunately I survived and spent nearly a year in hospital before I was well enough to be discharged.

Meningitis left me physically disabled. During my early years, not only did I have great difficulty in making myself understood, I was so uncoordinated that I had to be propped up against a wall with cushions, like Christy Brown in *My Left Foot*.

Although I do have some movement in my legs, since the age of four I've used a wheelchair to get about. I am therefore not a paraplegic, nor am I wheelchair-*bound* or *confined* to a wheelchair. I certainly don't see myself as a prisoner or a helpless victim of my disability.

For someone with special educational needs like myself, it was therefore vital that I was given every opportunity to make the most of my limited physical abilities and shine academically. Fortunately, my first taste of education was at the fairly enlightened Salters Lane Special School in Darlington, built in 1929, which catered solely for physically disabled youngsters between the ages of four and sixteen. It was also commonly known as the open air school because in the past it had exposed its so-called 'delicate' pupils, who were suffering from breathing disorders such as asthma or chronic bronchitis, to a regime of outdoor exercise, fresh air and sunlight, which it was thought would be beneficial to their health.

I entered the newly-opened nursery unit of the school in 1969 when I was only four years old, and I can vividly remember one of my very first lessons. I was sitting in a circle of children around a teacher, and she had a clock in her lap and was moving the hands to show us how to tell the time.

Despite my speech impediment, when it was my turn to speak I confidently proclaimed, 'Two o'clock', to which she replied, 'Good guess, Paul.' Clearly, she didn't believe that a boy of four could know the answer without having received prior instruction from her, but I already knew how to tell the time, even at that age. I had my father to thank for teaching me when I was only two and a half years old. Seeking further proof of my precocious ability, she altered the hands of the clock and asked me again. I said, 'Five o'clock.' This time she said I was lucky. But when she pointed at the clock on the classroom wall and I gave the correct answer for the third time, she rushed to fetch the headmaster to witness this miraculous event.

Unfortunately, my budding mental faculties were undermined by a lack of bodily control. I can recall, for example, with some embarrassment, being dropped off at home by the school minibus. When the lady pushed my wheelchair to the door she would hand my mother a small bundle and say, 'There's your parcel, Mrs Hodgson.' Inside was a pair of my soiled underpants, because I was frequently incontinent at that age and would have a supply of clean underclothes at the school so that I could be changed.

Home at that time was a two-bedroomed terraced house in Dundee Street, Darlington, which we extended so that I had a downstairs bathroom. When I was a little boy I had to be carried upstairs for a bath, which was a bit awkward to say the least, especially as I got older. Until I was seven I had to share a room with my twin sister Alison, but after that time I used the front room as my bedroom.

My family circumstances can be briefly recounted. My mother's maiden name was Alice Wood, and she was born in 1930 in Wakefield, West Yorkshire. Her mother died in 1942 when she was only twelve. After my mother left Ings Road Secondary Modern School in 1944 she started work at the Public Benefit Shoe Shop in Wakefield, but she didn't stay there long due to the low pay and poor working conditions. She went to work instead at Holdsworth Mill, which was only about a mile from where she lived, and remained there until she moved to Darlington in 1948. She worked at Pease's Mill in Darlington until she got married in 1950 to a local man.

My mother left her first husband in 1962, and the six children from that broken marriage were either fostered or ended up in local authority care. She set up home with my father in 1964 and a year later Alison and I were born.

By comparison with my stepbrother and stepsisters, Alison and I were brought up in a fairly stable, though far from ideal, environment. It became clear to me as I grew older that my mother and father had serious marital problems, and the fault line running through their relationship would frequently manifest itself in damaging rows. I don't know the reasons for this discord, and I wouldn't like to speculate on whether my disability had a part to play.

In September 1972 my parents decided that it would be beneficial if I went away as a boarder to what was then called the Percy Hedley Centre for Spastics in the Forest Hall area of Newcastle-upon-Tyne, now thankfully renamed the Percy Hedley Centre. Opened in 1953, the school was the largest of its kind in Europe, with over a hundred pupils.

It was then that I realised I was different from the other children in my street who went instead to the local schools, and when it was time for me to leave I didn't want to go. Even though I was lucky in that I had a good house mother at Percy Hedley called Elsie Ferguson, the transition from my home in Darlington to the alien environment of the special school in Newcastle was hard to come to terms with, especially at such a young age.

Until I moved to Percy Hedley my mother had done virtually everything for me, and that was a big mistake. She realised that later, but at that time she still used to dress and feed me. Naturally, I found it quite a strain at first being away from home. Also, in those early days I didn't come home very often at weekends, which didn't help matters. Even harder to bear was the fact that when I came home I was often on my own, because I lost daily contact with my friends in the neighbourhood simply by being away at school.

As I've already said, Elsie was a good house mother – strict but fair. But I hated those early years at Percy Hedley. It was the *feeling* of being on my own that I didn't like, even though in reality I was surrounded by fellow pupils and caring members of staff. So it was no surprise that I was lonely and didn't fit in. Consequently, I didn't make an effort in occupational therapy, speech therapy or physiotherapy. With the benefit of hindsight, I can see that I wasn't interested.

To increase my sense of isolation, I could hardly talk at that time; it was an effort to string two words together that were comprehensible. For example, when I visited relatives or friends my sister would usually speak up on my behalf. 'Paul likes bourbons' she'd say if she were offered some biscuits. (Though she was not averse to using this knowledge of my preferences to get the things that *she* liked!) My speech therefore remained undeveloped through lack of practice. For want of a better expression, I was a lazy little sod.

The object of going to a special school is to make you as independent as possible, and for me my schooldays certainly were a special time, since they gave me the opportunity to prepare for my future role in the adult world. As you can imagine, the teachers were quite tough, and in a way they had to be. However, although the discipline at Percy Hedley was severe, it was only with the object of making the pupils as self-reliant as possible. The cane was never used as a punishment. But I still wasn't making any effort in the classroom and got everyone to run after me, which wasn't the way to behave at all. Any progress I made was slow and painful. But I suppose a seven-year-old boy, wrenched from the family home, does have some semblance of an excuse.

Although my home life left a lot to be desired, at least I was around people that I knew. As I've mentioned before, I felt my father could never come to terms with my disability, so his absence was no great loss. Instead, it was my mother who I missed more than anybody in the world when I was at Percy Hedley. These feelings of homesickness were diminished, to a certain extent, by the letters and money that she used to send me.

At first my mother had been over-protective towards me, but she soon learnt the error of her ways. In no time at all her attitude had changed and she tried her best to teach me the importance of being resilient and self-sufficient. She would say to me, 'One day, Paul, I won't be here to look after you, that's why you have to be able to do as much for yourself as possible.'

But when I used to return at the weekend from boarding school things never seemed to be right at home, and my mother was unhappy for much of the time. My parents certainly seemed to be an ill-matched pair. In the early years of their marriage they would go out together at the weekend to Hopetown and Whessoe Working Men's Club, and my grandmother would come round to babysit. Eventually, my mother stopped going with him and so my father would go out on his own for a drink and to play darts with his mates.

Although my home life could have been happier I never wanted for anything in material terms, given the fact that my father had a reasonably well-paid labouring job with the Whessoe[2] in Darlington and my mother worked part-time in the town's indoor market on a leather goods store selling handbags and the like. Whatever the underlying cause of my parents' unhappiness might have been, it was definitely not due to a lack of money, though I should point out that my father's apparent reluctance to spend it certainly did give rise to ill-feeling and resentment.

Luckily, I discovered a place where I could escape from the family squabbles and even make new friends into the bargain. The name of this special place was Feethams, the home of Darlington Football Club, and because I was disabled I could get in for free, though the cynical reader might be forgiven for thinking that this should apply to all those foolhardy souls who venture into the ground and actually pay for the privilege! Little did I know it at the time that this would eventually become an all-consuming obsession.

The first game I saw at a fog-shrouded Feethams was on the 6th of January 1973 when I was only seven years old. Our visitors that day were Southport, who at the time were promotion contenders, while we were firmly rooted to the bottom of the league. Our home fixture against Workington on Boxing Day had already been postponed because a mixture of injuries and a flu epidemic had reduced Darlington to just eight fit players, and because of the foggy conditions the Southport game was only given the go-ahead by the referee an hour before kick-off.

The previous game on the 23rd of December 1972 was away to Bradford City where we were hammered 7-0. Apparently, after the game at Valley Parade the newly-installed Darlington manager, Ralph Brand, assured the press that the result had been a one-off, and that we would never be beaten like that again. However, the omens certainly didn't look good for the visit of Southport. Allan Jones, who had been sent on a three week 'holiday' by the chairman, George Tait, officially parted company with the football club

[2]A heavy-engineering company.

on the 21st of December. He became the fourth Darlington manager to lose his job in only fifteen months.

Worse was to follow on the day of the match. Phil Owers, a seventeen-year-old rookie goalkeeper, had the misfortune of being called upon to make his first team debut in place of Ernie Adams. Not that Phil disgraced himself – as a matter of fact he went on to carve out for himself a lengthy career in the professional game and only retired in February 1999, so that first appearance can't have been too traumatic.[3]

The match was certainly a one-sided affair. By half-time we were 4-0 down and we went on to lose 7-0, which is our heaviest ever home league defeat. To cap it all I'd pestered my mother for weeks to take me to a Darlington game! My abiding memory was, 'What the hell have I come down here for in the middle of winter in the freezing cold?'

Throughout the game, as the ball hit the back of the net with alarming regularity, Ralph Brand stayed in the directors' box instead of coming down to the touchline. His semi-detached attitude was exemplified by the fact that he actually lived in Edinburgh where he was in business and only commuted to Darlington each Wednesday where he remained until Saturday. At the final whistle the fans gave Phil Owers a standing ovation. After all, he wasn't to blame for the rout.

I bet that hasn't happened very often in professional football – two consecutive seven-nil defeats with two different goalkeepers. Those two results must have struck a chord with David Frost, who in February of that year highlighted our plight by making a documentary about the club. At the end of the season, which saw Southport crowned as champions of the old Fourth Division, the Quakers finished bottom and had to apply yet again for re-election at the Football League Annual General Meeting in June. Fortunately, we managed to retain our status with a majority of twelve votes over our nearest rivals, Yeovil Town.

Trust me to start supporting the club during our worst ever season in the Football League. Out of forty-six league games we won only seven, which was one fewer than our previous worst in season 1936-37.[4] So, after such a dismal introduction to life as a Darlington supporter, why did I come back for more?

Could it have been the smell of Bovril or pork pies, wafting towards me from the refreshment kiosk, which indelibly imprinted itself on my

[3]Cf. Harry Pearson's book *The Far Corner*, pp. 111-12, for an account of a 'silver-haired' Phil Owers playing for Shildon in 1993.

[4]We equalled that feat of winning only seven games in season 1986-87 when we were relegated from the Third to the Fourth Division.

consciousness? Perhaps I was eagerly awaiting the sound of an air horn to bring the team and the crowd to life. Maybe, though, it was the devoted fans standing on the North Terrace who captivated me, drumming out that incessant eleven beat pattern, like a Morse code message, on the resonant fabric of the so-called Tin Shed – dah, dah / dah, dah, dah / dah, dah, dah, dah / *Darlo*.

Surely it can't have been the quality of the football on offer that enthralled me? During the seventies we were well and truly anchored in the doldrums and had to make five re-election applications in just eleven seasons. Was I therefore simply a glutton for punishment? I suppose I must have thought, as football fans generally do when their team is faring badly, that things could only get better. And in that respect I was right.

With me being at Percy Hedley during the week I could only go to the Saturday fixtures, but it wasn't long before some of the players began to recognise me and came over for a chat prior to the kick-off. I can remember that Clive Nattress and Colin Sinclair did this fairly regularly.

After those early, difficult years at Percy Hedley I began to settle in, tried to do a lot more work and things started to improve for me. I still couldn't sit up properly, I still had awfully bad balance, and had to be propped up otherwise I would fall over. At the time I thought that would be the norm for me. It's funny how kids think like that. My support for the Quakers had, I suppose, predisposed me to adopt that stoical frame of mind. When, season after season, the team struggled to avoid re-election by the skin of their teeth that was what I had come to expect. So why should my own circumstances be any different?

Chapter 2

By the time I was eight years old, I began to take more of an interest in my surroundings. In my second year at Percy Hedley I tried quite hard and became friendly with a boy called Michael. Unlike me, he could walk, though he did have some mild learning difficulties. I, on the other hand, was quite bright, when I applied myself, though most of the time I just couldn't be bothered.

Even in my third year I was a lazy little bugger, but something happened to me then which really made me change my ways. I was kept back a full year because I wasn't trying. After that I did quite well academically. I also improved my mobility and posture as a result of going to physiotherapy sessions with a lady called Alison Carlisle, who knew I was capable of much more.

The physiotherapists also suggested that I should try out some special boots and callipers on my legs in an attempt to make them stronger. My mother and father agreed, and I remember the first day that I wore these strange contraptions, like some medieval torture device. They hurt like hell and so I threw them on the floor in disgust.

I have to thank Mrs Carlisle for her perseverance. She picked them up and put them back on for me. Eventually, rather than wobbling about on legs like jelly, I could actually walk, after a fashion, provided someone accompanied me, and I could sit up straight in a chair, unaided.

Even after so much improvement in my condition my mum used to have to pay my dad to drive me back home for the weekend in the family car. Although my mother and sister supported me, in his stubborn way my father still couldn't bring himself to show me any attention or praise my achievements. And it hurt for him not to take pride in his son's obvious improvement.

Not that my father was always disagreeable. Although he seemed mostly indifferent to me, there were times when he behaved like a considerate human being. Sometimes he would take me with him to places such as Ripon, Thirsk and Harrogate to release his beloved racing pigeons for what's known in the trade as a 'toss,' in other words a trial flight.

I should explain that my father is a pigeon fancier. At first he kept them in a loft at the back of our house, but after complaints from the neighbours he moved them to an allotment on Hundens Lane in Darlington. To this day I don't understand why my father bothered, because they very often failed to return after he released them. Despite spending considerable sums of money on his hobby, a rosette for first place usually eluded him. In fact, his pigeons reminded me of the Quakers during that dismal 1972-73 season – they hardly ever won! My grandfather claimed that this was because my father used to starve them. The reason that they didn't come back, he used to say, was because they stopped off in a cornfield for a bite to eat!

I must have been no more than nine or ten years old when my father took me with him in the car on a mission to recover one of his pigeons that had gone astray. It all started when someone found one of his birds, and after reading the details on the identification ring on its leg, the man telephoned Hopetown and Whessoe pigeon club. My father then contacted him and arranged a convenient time to pick it up. The two of us went in the car to a house in the Skerne Park area of Darlington. For the reader unacquainted with that part of town, I should explain that Skerne Park is a council estate, which, at the time, had a reputation for crime and problem families.

When we arrived at the address I sat in the car while my father went to the door. My first impressions of the area were hardly favourable: the front of the house looked like a council tip; there was a wrecked car standing on the lawn, surrounded by assorted junk, the grass was at least a foot high and there was no garden gate. When my father returned he said the interior was every bit as bad as the exterior. Apparently, the staircase and the gate had been chopped up and burnt on the fire – the occupants used a ladder to get upstairs and it seems that the copper water tank had been disconnected and sold to a scrap metal dealer!

Sometimes my father would take me into his confidence and tell me about his job at the Whessoe. Whether he was pulling my leg I don't know, but he certainly never tried to give me the impression that he was a model employee. Within our family it was common knowledge that, as a result of a bad back caused by an accident during his National Service days, he would regularly take time off work. Yet it was interesting that my father could always manage to lift heavy baskets of pigeons and dig the allotment over without any problem!

My father didn't share my love of football, and perhaps my total identification with the Quakers stemmed from a need to compensate for his behaviour towards me. Certainly, it would be no exaggeration to say that Darlington Football Club provided me with a place of refuge and became, in effect, a surrogate family for me.

When I started to support the team during the 1970s, apart from a few good cup runs, we were invariably struggling to avoid finishing in the bottom four. At the time I thought that was the norm. I can remember our last game against Swansea City on the 28th of April 1976 when a point was enough to avoid that fate. Stan Webb scored for the Quakers in the 65th minute and Swansea equalised five minutes from time. The celebrations after the final whistle were unbelievable – the players were dancing on the pitch and the fans were singing, 'We are the champions.' We had achieved our aim of not finishing in the bottom four and therefore having to apply for re-election. That was the limit of our ambition. Nowadays, a manager would be sacked if his team finished fifth from bottom of the table.

Despite our miserable record in the league, all through the 1970s I went to as many home games as I could. One of the highlights was being drawn against Sheffield Wednesday in the second round of the FA Cup at Feethams. After one postponement due to bad weather, we eventually played the tie on the 15th of December 1976.

The game was an ill-tempered affair and the start of the second half was even delayed for eight minutes after fighting broke out on the pitch between the rival sets of fans. With only minutes remaining Ron Ferguson unleashed a blistering shot from all of thirty yards into the top corner of the Wednesday net. The Owls had released Ron a few months previously, and I can recall him going over to the dugout after he had scored the winning goal and sticking two fingers up to Len Ashurst, the Wednesday manager at the time. I liked Ferguson after that. He was a big centre-forward who used to go in really hard. He was my kind of player!

By this time I was eleven years old and in the fourth year at Percy Hedley. I was no angel, far from it, and was always getting into trouble, though nothing serious, I hasten to add. I can remember one day I decided to run away. I'd simply had enough. A lad called Kevin and me packed our suitcases, but we didn't get very far, only half way up the road, as it happened. We ended up being severely reprimanded I can tell you.

Until I reached the age of eleven I shared a dormitory with six other lads. After that time I only had to share a room with another boy, which was much better. However, there was one drawback to this situation – the boy was often incontinent in his bed. The night carer, wearing surgical gloves, used to clean him up first with some sheets of toilet roll and then wash him down with a sponge and a bucket of soapy water. But rather than taking him somewhere else, she would do all this right in front of me, because his bed was just on the other side of the room from mine. The idea that I might not want to see this spectacle never even crossed her mind. It seemed to me that my privacy counted for nothing.

Over a period of two to three years my speech became a lot clearer. At first hardly anyone could understand what I was trying to say. I did have a bad speech impediment and was amazed at the marked improvement, which was down to my own hard work and the patience of my speech therapist. I also began to excel at my schoolwork and could now manage to walk using parallel bars or holding on to someone's waist, which I thought was one hell of an achievement. I was really proud of that. At twelve years of age I had reached my physical peak, so to speak.

I think too many disabled people don't make the effort to improve their lot. They're quite prepared to sit on their backside and mope about. But that wasn't how I envisaged my life as an adult. I wanted more than that and was determined to achieve a degree of independence.

So, by the time I was twelve I could wash and dress myself, clean my teeth and feed myself, things which my doctor said I would never be able to do. Now I only needed speech therapy about once a month, and I improved by reading aloud in bed, often from *Shoot!* magazine and other football-related publications. It is Lynne Birrell and Judith Booth who I have to thank for this. They both knew that I had a great deal of unrealised potential and gave me lots of encouragement. I also had a new physiotherapist called Gillian Miller who spurred me on even further.

Even when I was at school, my thoughts would often turn to the next match at Feethams. For instance, one of the highlights from this time was beating Fulham on the 5th of September 1978 in the second round of the League Cup to secure a tie with Everton at Goodison Park. Having drawn 2-2 at Craven Cottage, with Derek Craig and Dennis Wann getting our goals, Barry Lyons, the former Nottingham Forest star, got the only goal in the replay at a rainswept Feethams from the penalty spot in the 63rd minute after Terry Bullivant and Kevin Lock combined to bring down our winger, Lloyd Maitland. I actually skived off school for that Tuesday night game, and I can remember thinking that it was well worth the effort. Unfortunately, I couldn't go to the Everton match, which we narrowly lost 1-0 despite an excellent performance, though I did listen to the commentary on the radio. In fact Gordon Lee, the Everton manager, admitted that his team had only two hard games that season – one was against Liverpool and the other was against Darlington, which I thought was high praise indeed.

It was then that I entered the upper school where I studied subjects like Biology, English, Mathematics and History. One of my favourite subjects was Social Studies. What I particularly liked was that in the first year we used to visit old people in their homes. I befriended a man called Mr Arrol and I was the only person he would allow in to see him. He used to tell me about his exploits during the Second World War and I enjoyed going to see him.

My friendship with Mr Arrol and the pleasure we both derived from each other's company provided a stark contrast to that of my own father. As time went by *his* behaviour had become more and more objectionable. For example, one Christmas Eve Alison, my mum and dad and myself were playing cards. My dad was cheating and Alison spotted the deception. Since he brazenly denied Alison's accusation I said that I'd seen him as well. He then stood up, threw the cards on the floor and flung his Christmas present – a pair of shoes that my mother had bought him – in the general direction of the Christmas tree, which bore the brunt of his anger.

Academically, I was determined to succeed after wasting so much time in the junior school. One disadvantage though was that Percy Hedley included, in the same class, pupils with learning difficulties alongside people who were physically disabled. Since I was quite bright I sometimes felt that I was being held back, and as I got older I felt that I was being held back even more.

I should explain that in most special schools this practice has now stopped. Pupils with learning difficulties are no longer taught in the same class as the physically disabled, which I think is a big improvement. Quite a lot of people with learning difficulties can be rather disruptive and I found that a bit of a pain, especially in my last year of senior school when I was trying to study for my CSEs and people were mucking about in the classroom with paper aeroplanes. That really wasn't my scene.

On the football front, season 1980-81 brought an upturn in the Quakers' fortunes as John Stalker and Alan Walsh's forty goals between them propelled us up to eighth in the league. ('Walshy' is still the club's all time record goal scorer with exactly 100 league and cup goals in 271 full appearances.) And I was lucky to be in the ground on the day that we became the first ever club in the country to officially stage a Sunday fixture in the Football League when we played Mansfield Town in February 1981.[1] With national television and press coverage focussed on the game our average gate of 2,500 had swelled to an impressive 5,932. According to Mike Amos in *The Northern Echo*, the club printed two thousand programmes and bought a thousand pies, all of which they sold! After Ian Hamilton converted a penalty, Mansfield scored twice and we needed a rare headed goal in the 88th minute from Alan Walsh to earn us a 2-2 draw.

[1]Quakers fans might be interested to know that Les McJannet played for the Stags that day.

At the time I was going out with a girl called Kerry who was a fellow pupil at Percy Hedley and who lived in Newcastle. She was my first real girlfriend. One day in April 1981 I invited her to stay at my house for the weekend. I was lying on top of the bed, fondling her, when I saw Alison's face peering at me through a gap in the bedroom curtains. She knocked on the window and said, 'You dirty little bugger!' then blackmailed the two of us by saying that unless Kerry handed over her Adam and the Ants album she would tell my mother what she had seen.

I tried to make it up to Kerry by taking her to the home fixture against Torquay on the Sunday. Despite having lots of pressure the game remained goalless until with only five minutes to go Quakers were awarded a corner kick. David Speedie floated the ball to the near post where it was touched on to my hero Kevan Smith, who headed home the winner from almost on the goal line. This was Kevan's first goal of that season.

Kerry and I eventually went our separate ways after about a year together. However, I should explain that my first actual sexual experience was at Percy Hedley itself. Elsie had left me alone in the bathroom when I heard a knock at the door. Before I could say anything, a trainee on the Youth Opportunities Programme came in and closed it behind her. Then she asked me, in a rather suggestive manner, if I needed a hand. I said I was fine but she just smiled, leaned over the bath and started masturbating me. I was so shocked that I just let her do it. Then she drained some of the water out of the bath, pulled down her knickers and got on top of me. After it was all over, she calmly walked out of the room without so much as a word being said. The whole episode must have lasted only ten minutes because shortly afterwards Elsie returned. When I passed the girl in the corridor the next day she just smiled and said, 'Hello, Paul.' It was as if the encounter hadn't even taken place.

I left school in 1981 with four CSE passes at Grade 2 in Arithmetic, English Literature, English Language Written and English Language Oral. I've mentioned previously my lack of coordination which makes writing out of the question – all I can manage is a shaky scrawl. You will also realise that nineteen years ago computers were not as familiar in the school environment as they are today, so when I came to take my exams I used a standard electric typewriter, fitted with a device called a keyguard, to ensure that I pressed only one key at a time. Since this was a laborious business, the examiners allowed me extra time to complete my papers.

Out of a class of fifteen or sixteen pupils only four of us took CSEs. The rest of them weren't up to it. That was a shame really. I was only given the opportunity to sit four exams and yet I passed them all without any problem. I know now that these passes would be considered by many people as pretty awful, but I came out with a lot more than the other pupils did.

If I had to voice a criticism of Percy Hedley it would be that too much emphasis was placed on acquiring independent living skills such as personal hygiene at the expense of social skills. In my view, learning how to interact with the rest of the non-disabled world and studying for academic qualifications would have been more useful in finding employment later on in life. That apart, I have nothing but praise for the school and its dedicated staff.

After an interview with the careers adviser at Percy Hedley he recommended a college of further education called The National Star Centre in Cheltenham, but it wasn't for me and so I turned down the opportunity because I didn't feel that it was the right thing to do at that moment in time. My mother in particular was bitterly disappointed by my refusal to continue with my studies, but I solemnly promised her that one day I would return to education.

Chapter 3

When I left Percy Hedley in 1981 I got my Green Card from the Manpower Services Commission, which meant that I could register for employment and was eligible for certain welfare benefits. Despite being unemployed for most of the 1980s, I was able to manage on my income from the state, topped up by my Mobility Allowance. Quite apart from the £15 a week I paid towards my board, I still had sufficient spending money to watch football when I pleased and go out drinking at the weekend.

As luck would have it, work and pleasure became one and the same thing for me after I met Barry Wetherill, the chairman of Darlington FC Supporters' Club. At the time he was in business as a florist, and his shop in Grange Road also served as a booking office for people who wanted to travel on the supporters' coach to away matches. Barry and I were soon good friends and used to go out drinking together.

When Barry offered me the post of Order Clerk for the Supporters' Club I gladly accepted. For the next six years I sold hats, scarves, badges and other football-related merchandise from home, getting orders from as far afield as the USA. Strictly speaking though, I was still unemployed, because I was working on a voluntary, unpaid basis.

Working for the Supporters' Club and being a member of the committee gave me the opportunity to become more directly involved with Darlington FC. Consequently, this meant that I went on many away trips with Barry. My friendship even extended to going on holiday with him, his wife and their daughter during the close season. He certainly liked the West Coast of Scotland, and between 1982 and 1986 the four of us went to such far-flung destinations as the Isle of Mull, Mallaig and Altby.

During this period of my life I met quite a lot of decent people, some of whom, like Barry, became good friends. It is these football friendships that I intend to mention in the following pages.

When I started to travel with Barry in season 1981-82 I went to six away games in total, all of which we lost. Perhaps the most memorable was in March 1982 when we played Rochdale at Spotland. Quakers twice threw away the lead that day. Dale grabbed their winner in the last few minutes when Kevan Smith played a woefully short back pass to his keeper, Pat Cuff, which Mark Hilditch intercepted, rolling the ball into the unguarded net The final score was 3-2, with David Speedie[1] getting both our goals, but it was

[1]Speedie was sold to Chelsea for a then club record fee of £65,000 in the summer of 1982. My friend Gavin Ellis arranged for me to be presented with his old number six Darlington shirt, which I still have to this day.

what happened off the pitch that sticks in my mind, rather than the game itself.

Because he was unable to take me himself, Barry had arranged for a helper from Darlington Supporters' Club to accompany me on the coach and push my wheelchair to the ground. Since the coach arrived in Rochdale well before the kick-off, we went for a drink in the Supporters' Social Club behind the Main Stand.

While we were there, a full-scale riot broke out, during the course of which a skinhead came up to me and asked, very politely, 'Do you mind if I take this table?' mine being the only one left intact. Not wishing to see my glass of lager lying smashed at my feet, I replied, 'Let me have a drink first,' and so he said, 'No problem, Paul.' Although he obviously knew me by name, I didn't know him from Adam. He then lifted up my table and clobbered some poor unfortunate Rochdale supporter over the head with it!

I can remember seeing the same skinhead later, lying flat on his back with his mouth wide open, drinking beer from the tap on the bar. The barmaid tried to prevent him with cries of 'No, no, stop it!' but she was just crudely told to fuck off. One lad became honorary barman and proclaimed, 'Drinks on the house, today!' while others simply clambered over the bar and helped themselves. As for me, I sat there calmly supping away at my half of lager in all that mayhem. It was like being in the eye of a storm.

A well-aimed kick from a Doctor Marten boot smashed the Supporters' Club trophy cabinet, and the looters paraded the cups and shields as if they had just received them after a Wembley Cup Final victory. Some of the other louts held a competition to see who could shit in the pockets of the snooker table! Another lad nicked the snooker balls, probably to use them later as missiles – you could see them bulging in his trouser pockets. In short, they absolutely wrecked the place.

The police didn't show up for at least half an hour, by which time the culprits had vanished, and because there were no video cameras installed on the premises no prosecutions were ever brought. After the hooligans had left, the barmaid said, 'I've never seen such dirty bastards before in all my life,' and she was certainly right on that score.

This was my first ever experience of actual football violence, with the possible exception of the game against Sheffield Wednesday in 1976, and in some ways I quite enjoyed the excitement of it all. Although I certainly don't condone what happened, the events of that day were like some puerile comedy, which I must say I found amusing at the time and also in retrospect.

I should add that my helper sat beside me, rigid with fear, throughout the entire commotion. Perhaps what he witnessed that day put him off for good because I certainly never saw him again!

When I was on the Supporters' Club committee for the first time we organised a night out. This was during the 1982-83 season. Kevan Smith talked me into coming along too, so I went to the pub with Barry. All the players got really drunk that night. One of them was on the stage, naked, with a pink ribbon round his dick and two strippers were fondling him. I expect that player will be glad if I don't mention him by name!

The following day word reached the manager about the events that night. As I was almost an unofficial ambassador of the club, I was summoned to his office and told I was a disgrace for being only seventeen and going to a pub where strippers were performing on stage. While the manager, Billy Elliott, was reprimanding me, Kevan Smith was standing behind him, taking the mickey. I tried my best to keep a straight face at his antics, but eventually I just couldn't help myself and burst out laughing. Billy Elliott, who didn't know what was going on behind his back, said sternly, 'It's not funny, boy,' and told me to get out. As a result of my indiscretion, I was banished from the precincts of the club for a week. In fairness to Billy Elliott, I must say that he always treated me well and was a really nice guy, so I was disappointed when he was sacked at the end of the season.

In the early 1980s CB radio was all the rage, rather like the Internet is today, and I was one of those who embraced the new medium. I was able to converse with people and make friends on an equal footing – over the airwaves they couldn't tell that I was disabled and used a wheelchair. All they could hear from my voice was that I stammered.

Some time during 1983 I struck up a conversation with a girl called Sandra: my handle was, appropriately enough, 'Quaker Star,' though hers shall remain a secret. After talking for about three weeks we decided to meet. From then on she used to come round to my house and we would go down town together. We saw each other for about five months altogether.

Her parents, though, didn't approve of our relationship. My being disabled ensured that they just couldn't see past the wheelchair. This was my first experience of prejudice and it was something I was going to become familiar with over the next few years. Sandra's parents put more and more pressure on her until she ended the relationship. I felt really bad at the time, but I eventually got over it and carried on with my life.

Season 1983-84 saw Darlington appoint a new manager, Cyril Knowles, but the improvement in our league position was only slight, and we eventually finished fourteenth. Altogether, I went to thirteen away games that season, mostly with Stephen Lowson. I first met Stephen at a home match in September 1983. We then went together to see the team play away at Stockport County in October of that year (a two-nil defeat) and became good friends from then on.

Stephen also used to visit me at least two or three times a week since we were both unemployed. To keep ourselves amused we would go on the CB radio or we would play board games like *Scrabble* and *Monopoly*. Stephen usually beat me at *Scrabble*, so I would resort to cheating, using abbreviations like TV when I was desperate for the points! On another occasion we even drafted a spoof letter to *The Sun's* agony aunt, full of the crudest sexual fantasies which, not surprisingly, didn't find its way into print.

Whenever Stephen came round my mother would make dinner for us and even bake cakes. The two of us would have competitions to see who could cram the most currant buns, jam tarts or scones in his mouth at once. After the meal a running joke would involve me telling my mother that Stephen had said the food was bloody awful and that she'd have to do a lot better next time, at which my mother would always smile.

My dad, though, kept himself to himself, practising for hours on end in front of a dartboard that he had set up in the living room. He was certainly a good player and his one claim to fame was that he had once beaten the former world darts champion, John Lowe.

The only time Stephen would actually see my father was when he would barge into my bedroom unannounced and turn off the gas fire. His stinginess at this time was legendary, especially when it came to his fixation with the gas bill. He would read the meter every week with a clipboard in his hand and would charge me a fixed sum of £3 per week, summer or winter. In the colder months if you ever happened to walk into the living room while my father was there you'd see him sitting in his hat and coat with the gas fire set on miser rate, just so that he could save a few measly quid. Once, he actually told my sister to turn it down in case the rug caught fire!

This was just one noticeable example of his misplaced prudence. Not only did he keep a tight rein on the purse strings, for several years running he gave my mother the same birthday card, which he hid in a wardrobe. No wonder she needed to go out to work to make ends meet, because when it came to birthday or Christmas presents it was naturally my mother who bought them. My father would even charge me fifty pence just to take me to the football! My abiding image is of him sitting there with his palm face upwards, waiting for the fare, and yet if it hadn't have been for my being disabled he wouldn't have got a free tax disc for his car in the first place.

In March 1984 Darlington played Bristol City away.[2] As Barry got me on board the Intercity 125 train early on Saturday morning at Darlington's Bank Top station, we soon realised that we would be sitting in the same coach as the players. Having lifted me into a vacant seat, Barry stowed my folded wheelchair in the luggage area near the coach door, and I found myself sitting opposite the club captain, Dave McLean. When he suggested a game of cards, another player called John Hannah came to make a foursome with Barry and me. I can remember that we played three-card brag and that Cyril Knowles watched us from a distance.

To my surprise, I ended up winning handsomely. In our final game the stake crept up inexorably from 50p, to £1, to £5 and then to £10 until I mischievously increased it to £50. By this time the pot contained well over £100 and John Hannah would have needed £50 just to see me, so he threw in his strong hand of three queens. My bluff had worked. When he saw me scooping up the pot with my miserable hand of ten high he quite understandably exclaimed, 'You bastard!'

At the time, John, who worked part-time as a pit electrician in the Yorkshire coalfield, was on strike. He joined us in October 1983 as a non-contract player, serving us well as a burly no-nonsense centre-forward, and was released in September 1984. In many ways his aggressive style of play reminded me of Ron Ferguson. Anyway, I felt guilty about taking so much money from him, especially as he was on strike, so I gave him a £30 backhander and he thanked me for being a gentleman.

When we arrived at Bristol Temple Meads station the players got a coach to the ground. Cyril offered to give us a lift but rather than have the hassle of carrying me on board the coach we thanked him and caught a taxi instead. The match turned out to be a great disappointment, with the home side well on top, the Robins forcing thirteen corners to the Quakers one. Six minutes from time we were denied a point when Keith Curle's cross dropped to the right foot of Trevor Morgan, who made no mistake. John Hannah on the other hand missed an absolute sitter when he completely miscued his shot. After what happened on the train, I suppose it just wasn't going to be his day! Although we came back on the same train as the players they were down in the dumps after their defeat, so we left them to it.

If we weren't watching football together, Stephen and I would usually go out drinking during the day or hang around Darlington town centre. Our

[2]Coincidentally, our top scorer, Alan Walsh, who didn't play that day because he was injured, was eventually sold to Bristol City in the summer of 1984 for a paltry £18,000, the fee set by tribunal.

favourite pubs were the Boot and Shoe, the Nag's Head, the Golden Cock and the Pied Piper. At that time I only drank halves, as a way of reducing my expenditure, whereas Stephen always drank pints. Stephen therefore nicknamed me 'Half-pint Hodgie.'

On one occasion we had been out on the beer and were bored, so we decided to go for a wander in Boyes department store. Rather than using the customer lift at the back of the store to get to the first floor, we went on the escalator instead. Stephen managed to do this without endangering my safety because he has a knack of balancing my wheelchair using his body as a counterweight. As we rode up the escalator we hummed the *Star Trek* theme tune rather loudly. Not surprisingly, some disgruntled members of staff ejected us pretty smartly.

We certainly had some adventures together. One night in a pub called the Pennyweight a woman came over to me and said, 'Excuse me, but me and my friends have just been wondering ... how do *you* have sex?' I looked at Stephen and could tell by his expression that he was shocked, so I said to her, 'I'll tell you what, darling, why don't you come in the bog with me now and I'll show you.' My frankness must have alarmed her because she just walked away. I suppose her insensitive enquiry amounted to sheer ignorance on her behalf; she genuinely couldn't imagine a man in a wheelchair actually having a sex life.

Another amusing incident in the company of Stephen occurred when I was sitting outside a betting shop. Gambling on the horses was another vice we indulged in at that time, though only small sums of money were ever involved. I would have been about nineteen at the time. Anyway, an old lady rustling a paper bag approached me and asked Stephen, 'Does the little boy want a sweetie?' I was utterly amazed. Just because I was in a wheelchair she thought I was a baby. I held back my anger and was determined to be polite, not obnoxious. Stephen, however, replied, 'Why don't you ask him, then.' This was just the invitation the old woman needed: first of all she patted me on my head, which is a fatal mistake, then instead of talking to me as an adult she forced one of those horrible black bullets into my mouth and said, 'There, there, little boy, you have a sweetie.' But I spat it out and said, 'No, the little boy doesn't want a sweetie, now fuck off.'

Chapter 4

Only four Darlington fans in a Ford Capri made the 350-mile journey to Torquay in September 1984, and I was one of them. To make matters worse, the match was an evening kick-off so we had to set off at about ten in the morning. Stopping twice at service stations en route, we arrived in Torquay at about five o'clock, and after some fish and chips to line our stomachs we sank a few pints in a pub near the ground.

When we entered Plainmoor, we discovered to our surprise that we were the only Darlington fans in the away end! That day we saw Steve Tupling and Willie Young, the former Scottish international, make their debuts for the Quakers. Although we forced fourteen corners to the home side's five, that was a misleading statistic. The Gulls scored after only ten minutes and hit the post twice. By contrast, we played abysmally and were lucky to be only 1-0 down. Torquay were so much the better side that if it had been a boxing match the referee would have intervened and stopped it. But we hung on gamely, got a corner with three minutes to go, which was taken by Dave McLean, the ball was flicked on at the near post by Colin Ross and Carl Airey gleefully headed in the equaliser. All I can remember is jumping up and down celebrating the goal as the Torquay supporters were predictably singing, 'You're going to get your fucking heads kicked in.' I think they must have been quite upset, because two policemen had to escort us back to our car for our own safety.

On the way back home we bumped into Cyril Knowles at a service station. When he saw how cramped the conditions were in the car he said, 'My God, you lot look squashed in there! Do you want me to take Paul with us?' I accepted his offer, and Kevan Smith carried me on board the team coach. This was the first time that I'd met Cyril, and from then on we became good friends. I sat with him at the front of the coach and we chatted for the rest of the journey. He admitted that we'd been very lucky that day, but as he said, it's the sign of a good side that can play below par and still come away with a draw. When we arrived in Darlington at three or four in the morning my friend Gavin Ellis was waiting for me outside Feethams and the driver of the Ford Capri gave me a lift back home.

Also in the West Country the game against Exeter City at the end of October springs to mind. Barry went to the railway station to negotiate a reduction in the fare for a party booking since there were not enough fans wanting to go to make it worthwhile hiring a coach for the long journey to Devon. As the train pulled out of Bank Top station we realised that one lad called Darren was missing from our group. 'Maybe he changed his mind at the last minute,' I suggested.

When we arrived at Exeter Barry was in the mood for some Gothic architecture so he pushed me the short distance from the station to the cathedral of the Blessed Virgin Mary and St Peter. Throughout my enforced sightseeing tour I was bored out of my mind and gagging for a drink! After the game, Stephen and Gavin naturally made fun of me for going to the cathedral with Barry.

The game itself was an eventful affair. Our goalkeeper, Fred Barber, saved a seventh minute penalty kick and Garry MacDonald scored on his debut with a tame shot from the edge of the area on thirty-four minutes. Exeter equalised seven minutes from the end to earn themselves a 1-1 draw. But with only five minutes of the match remaining, Stephen pointed at a lone figure trudging towards us and said, 'Isn't that Darren?' Apparently, he'd slept in, caught a later train, knowing that it wouldn't arrive in time for the game, and had paid full price for his ticket. Now there's true commitment for you!

After the match the police dropped us off at the train station and promptly left. Ten minutes later around one hundred Exeter fans arrived at the scene. We were sitting there having a quiet cup of coffee when we heard one of them say, 'Let's get the one in the wheelchair,' whereupon all hell broke loose. They chased the seventeen Darlington fans all over the platform, and during the course of this skirmish Stephen was slightly hurt.

One lad called Bob was even chased over the railway line. He was carrying some cans of lager in a plastic carrier bag and they all fell out. An Exeter thug offered him a derisory two pence for his Darlington scarf, but he declined, whereupon the lad took it from him by force. I suppose it would have made a good souvenir.

Another strange situation occurred when Darlington played Peterborough away in November 1984. Once again, I went on the train with Barry, but this time with the understanding that we weren't going to visit any more cathedrals!

I vividly remember that we just happened to be walking past a town centre pub when, without warning, a stool came crashing through the window. Within seconds it was like one of those wild-west saloon brawls you see in the movies. To our amazement the two sets of fans stopped fighting to let us past; it was like pressing the pause button on a video recorder. As soon as we had got past, they carried on fighting as if nothing had happened.

Some four hundred Darlington fans had made the journey to London

Road. Once we got inside the ground, it wasn't long before violence flared up again. After two minutes part of a small group of Darlington fans insisted on walking on the pitch as they were being ushered away from the home end. As the police were escorting them to the away enclosure one of them was hit on the head with, of all things, a milk crate! The Darlington fans in the Moys Terrace, incensed by this incident, scaled the perimeter fence and ran across the pitch towards the home fans. The game therefore had to be stopped for about five minutes so that mounted police could restore order and clear the pitch. Although Posh scored on forty-five minutes the game finished a 1-1 draw. Incidentally, Dave McLean scored our equaliser direct from a corner kick, although *The Northern Echo's* match report credits defender Martin Pike with the goal.

The following month Darlington played away at Stockport County. For some unfathomable reason Barry committed the fatal mistake of putting me in charge of the Supporters' Club coach. Now that really was an error of judgement on his part! He even insisted that I shouldn't allow any alcohol on board, so to keep him happy I promised that I wouldn't. At this time I should explain that there was a voluntary ban on alcohol on football coaches. Of course this was a barefaced lie because the very first thing I did was to make sure that we went to an off-licence and got stocked up with cans of beer and lager. By the time we arrived at Edgley Park two hours later we'd all had a skinful.

Carl Airey, our leading scorer, was serving a two-match ban that day, so it didn't come as a great surprise that the game finished a 0-0 draw on what was a frozen pitch. Despite only getting one point, the result sent the Quakers to the top of the table.

On the way back I was bursting for a leak so a lass held my plastic bottle for me while I urinated in it. But the bottle overflowed and some of the contents were spilled on the floor of the bus. On the basis of 'Monkey see, monkey do' some lads followed my example. Consequently, by the time we reached Darlington the bus stank to high heaven and the poor driver justifiably complained to the Supporters' Club about our behaviour.

On the 5th of January 1985 the Quakers were drawn against Middlesbrough at Ayresome Park in the third round of the FA Cup. I went there on the train with Stephen and as he pushed me along Linthorpe Road we naturally stopped off at a few pubs on the way. When we got to the ground the stewards gave Stephen a hand to carry me up into one of the seats. I seem to remember that it was a bitterly cold afternoon and the pitch was covered in snow.

As for the game itself, I'm still convinced that Garry MacDonald scored a perfectly valid goal that day, but the referee adjudged that the ball hadn't crossed the line. Mick Saxby, the Boro defender, claimed to have hacked it away from the muddy goalmouth, but it was well over the line in my opinion.

Three days later we played Middlesbrough in the replay at Feethams, and the game only went ahead after loyal fans turned up in their droves to clear two inches of snow from the pitch. Because of the demand for tickets, Stephen stood in the Tin Shed and I had to go in one of the East Stand seats – my usual spot in the paddock wouldn't have afforded much of a view with so many bodies in front of me. Darlington printed 5,000 programmes at forty pence each, although this time *The Northern Echo* didn't mention how many pies they bought!

Spurred on by a crowd of 14,237 we won the game 2-1, through goals by Garry MacDonald and Phil Lloyd, in spite of a certain amount of trouble as the Middlesbrough fans invaded the pitch in a vain attempt to get the game abandoned when we were 2-0 up. They only succeeded in getting the match held up for ten minutes. Concrete slabs and iron spikes were hurled at the police after a twenty-yard section of the perimeter fencing behind one of the goals collapsed. Altogether there were fifteen arrests and three people were taken to hospital.

It was also ironic that both Darlington goalscorers were former Boro players. When Tony McAndrew pulled one back for the Boro we had to endure a frantic last ten minutes before the referee blew the final whistle. The Boro fans vandalised the cricket pitch on their way out of the ground. In fact, they fought a running battle with rival fans on the cricket pitch, and it spilled out into Darlington town centre. I also heard that they set a railway carriage on fire as they made their way home, ripping out the seats and smashing the light fittings. The fire brigade were even called out to Middlesbrough railway station. They were definitely sore losers.

That second season under Cyril Knowles was certainly an eventful one. The next match I'd like to mention was at Bury in March 1985. Instead of using the supporters' coach, Barry took me there in his car along with two of the directors' wives. We arrived at the ground at about six o'clock, and since the two women preferred to head for the directors' box Barry and I went drinking in Bury instead.

When we returned to Gigg Lane in time for the kick-off we discovered that it was pitch dark inside the ground because there was obviously a problem with the electricity supply. Even though the floodlights were working, no doubt because they were powered by a separate generator, the scene in the bar was a different story – an old biddy was faffing about in the till looking for loose change, her only source of light some flickering candles.

Unfortunately, Barry and I were separated as we entered the ground and on this occasion I was put in the home end where a drunk decided to throw a punch at me. Although I managed to duck I lost my balance in the process and fell out of my wheelchair. Within a few seconds a dozen lads were putting the boot in. When the Darlington fans saw what was happening they ran across the pitch towards me. There I was, lying on the terraces, with a battle going on all around me. It was a frightening experience and one I'll never forget. I ended up with two cracked ribs. My mother pleaded with me not to go any more, but I was determined not to let the hooligans win. Much more worrying for me was the fact that when Hill scored the only goal of the match for the Shakers on sixty-eight minutes, the Quakers had their lead at the top of the table cut to two points.

After the game Barry and the two directors' wives were shocked by the severity of my injuries. As a precaution I went to Darlington Memorial Hospital on my return for a check up, and my cracked ribs were strapped up. I could have pressed charges against the hooligan who assaulted me but I decided not to. Although it was painful at the time, it wasn't the sort of thing that was going to stop me travelling to see the Quakers in action. Even the result couldn't shake my belief in the team.

In May 1985, I went to Crewe for the last away game of the season. Gavin put me on board the coach because Stephen had broken his leg playing football in Darlington's South Park. However, despite having his leg in plaster up to his thigh, Stephen still managed to push my wheelchair to the ground, which was quite a feat of dexterity on his part! This was also the first game I went to with Ian Carter, who was destined to become a very close friend. Little did I know that I would end up being best man at his wedding some seven years later.

Carl Airey scored both our goals on five and then twenty-five minutes to bring his tally to eighteen for the season, and even Kevan Smith got on the scoresheet after fifteen minutes (albeit at the wrong end!) Waller scored the equaliser for Crewe on eighty-five minutes, and I should add that David Platt played for the Railwaymen that day. I had a massive Darlington flag with me and I waved it for the whole of the first half. By that time my arms were killing me so I conned Ian into waving it for me. I kept telling him to hold it higher and by the end of the match he could hardly move his arms.

At the end of the game, having clinched promotion to the old Third Division, all the players threw their shirts into the crowd. I caught Mark

Forster's but some moron wrenched it out of my hand and it was gone.[1] Stephen, with the pot on his leg, climbed the fence to get a better view of the celebrations. I can still see him now, hanging by one leg on the fence, absolutely lapping up the occasion. Ian lifted me up too so that I could see what was happening on the pitch, but unfortunately while I was standing up someone stole the programme from my seat.

The final memory from the end of that season is of sitting in a service station, eating a meal, when there was a sudden roar: the Darlington team bus had stopped there as well. Everyone started singing and Cyril Knowles came over and had a long chat with me. We spoke about the game and about the season as a whole. That is the thing I loved about Cyril, he would always give you the time of day.

The players themselves were mobbed by the fans and spent three or four hours just talking and signing autographs. They all had time to come and talk to you because they knew how much it meant to the supporters. Some players don't have time for the fans, and that's sad. If it wasn't for them paying their admission money every week and supporting the club financially the players would be out of a job, especially in the lower divisions.

I remember going home thinking, 'I'm only twenty and I've seen us get promotion whereas some people have supported this club for years and have seen only mediocrity.' As a matter of fact, the last time we were promoted from the old Fourth Division was in season 1965-66 when we finished level on points with Doncaster, so it had been a long wait for some fans. This time we finished third, one point behind Blackpool and one point ahead of Bury.

During the close season, when there was no football to watch, I went with Stephen on a day trip to Redcar Races. Since he still hadn't recovered from his broken leg, you can imagine the scenario. There he was with his leg completely encased in plaster up to the thigh, trying to push a wheelchair. Not surprisingly, we got some funny looks along the way. True to form, we also visited a few pubs before we actually got to the racecourse.

After much deliberation, we decided to do a bet called a 'place pot', but our first horse went down, and we ended up having a terrible day on the gambling front. As a last resort, Stephen suggested that we should put the remainder of our stake money on the odds-on favourite to recoup the money that we'd lost. So we did just that and, would you believe it, the horse came

[1]Strangely enough, some fourteen years later, I bumped into Mark Forster at a Darlington FC reunion. In the course of our conversation, I happened to mention this incident. When he heard my tale he promised to give me a signed shirt from the period in question. True to his word, he posted the shirt through my letterbox the following day.

in second!

We still had a few quid left, so we decided to sample the pubs in Redcar town centre near the railway station. However, instead of pushing me the long way round the ring road, Stephen was adamant that he was going to use some steps because it was raining heavily. You can imagine him with the pot on his leg trying to manoeuvre me down those steps! Obviously, the inevitable happened; I fell arse over tip out of the wheelchair and we both collapsed in a heap together. Since I was relatively unharmed after my fall I started laughing, which set Stephen off as well. The way that he fell on top of me also made it look as if we were having sex, which was definitely not the case, I can assure you.

Anyway, a little old lady came to investigate, asking if she could help in any way. We could only lie there laughing hysterically and she walked off in disgust at our antics. Our shambolic appearance that day proved to be an apt foretaste of the Quakers' inept performances on the field of play at the start of the forthcoming football season.

Chapter 5

You'll have gathered by now that football abounds with well-intentioned fanatics like myself. Although there won't be many Darlington fans with a programme collection to rival mine, you'll be able to find fans of other clubs whose collections are even more impressive. And although I'm pretty well-informed about the history of the Quakers, there are always other fans who can reel off names, dates and scores much faster and with far greater accuracy than me.

Others aim to become members of the 92 Club[1] by seeing a first-team match played on all of the current English Premier and Football League grounds – their bible is Simon Inglis's book *Football Grounds of Britain*. There are also the 'ground-hoppers,' many of whom come over from the Continent, who spend their free time scouring the country, trying to fit in as many matches as possible. Like trainspotters collecting rare train numbers, they ceaselessly go about their work. In addition, there are the inevitable autograph hunters and football groupies who pursue players with the same degree of single-mindedness.

By and large, these are a harmless bunch of people. More typical are the ordinary fans, who make up the majority of supporters at any football club. Take my friends Bev and Rod, for example.

As a result of my job with the Supporters' Club, I received a letter from a lady called Bev who lived in Eastleigh, Hampshire. She wanted to buy some souvenirs, so I obliged and then asked if she'd consider writing to me as a penpal. When she wrote back I discovered that she originated from Barnard Castle and that her boyfriend, Rod, was a Southampton fan.

During the following two seasons Stephen and I stayed at Bev and Rod's house when Darlington were playing away at Bournemouth. Many's the time I've collapsed unconscious on their kitchen floor after a night out at their local, the Welcome Inn. Although they later split up, I did keep in touch with Rod until fairly recently – he was a guest at my thirtieth birthday party – and I often wonder how Bev is doing now.

My friendship with Bev and Rod was in marked contrast to that of another couple called Clare and Malcolm. If football can bring out the best in people, in terms of hospitality, loyalty and acts of kindness, it can also be responsible for some of the worst aspects of human behaviour. This was certainly the case with Clare and Malcolm.

My tale begins in 1985. Malcolm was just one of a group of lads including

[1]Founded in 1978.

a chap called Mark who went out drinking together in Darlington. Even then, Malcolm struck me as being rather odd and tight-fisted. When Clare came on the scene she started to go to away games with us, and in those days she always paid her whack.

On one of my trips on the supporters' coach, I introduced Clare and Malcolm to each other. Malcolm soon started to come to away games with us in Clare's car. At first I used to sit in the front seat of her car, which was a two-door saloon, but when Malcolm came with us he asked me to sit in the back, which was rather awkward to say the least. At first Clare would charge reasonable prices for these trips – a fiver each for example. But everything changed when Malcolm appeared. From then on Clare became as tight-fisted as her boyfriend and all of a sudden the prices shot up. We were also annoyed to see them arrive at a ground and then go straight inside in case they had to buy a round of drinks. This became almost a regular occurrence.

The Third Division, as I've already suggested at the end of Chapter Four, proved a greater test of our mettle, especially without the services of Kevan Smith to shore up our defence ('Smudger' was sold to Rotherham in the close season). Not surprisingly, by the time we played York City at Bootham Crescent in October 1985 we were already bottom of the league.

In the early hours of Saturday morning vandals had managed to get into the ground and broke the crossbar of one of the goals. Before the game Darlington fans went on the rampage in York city centre, smashing windows and brawling. Trouble also flared up during the match and altogether there were thirty arrests for public order offences that day.

Stephen, Ian, Malcolm, Clare and I made the half-hour trip to York by train. I remember that we arrived there at eleven o'clock, in other words opening time, and I got absolutely plastered. We even went to a quite posh restaurant for a meal. When I noticed a woman wearing a hat with artificial fruit on it at another table I couldn't help singing, 'Where did you get that hat, where did you get that hat?' only to be roundly rebuked.

After the meal we resumed our pub-crawl, and by the time we got to the ground I was laughing like a madman. Because of my state, the game was just an alcoholic blur. I later found out that Paul Ward was sent off for the Quakers after twenty-four minutes. York City's Tony Canham scored a hat-trick, Keith Walwyn got two and Steve Senior and Keith Houchen weighed in with a goal apiece. After the match, I honestly thought that we had won seven-nil, not the other way around! All the lads were naturally devastated by the result and there I was laughing. One of them said, 'Paul, what are you laughing at?' So I told him that it was because we'd won seven-nil. He replied, 'You daft bastard, we *lost* seven-nil, where the hell have you been.' After the game police with dogs escorted the four hundred Darlington fans to the railway station.

One day, as Clare's car pulled up outside my house it was raining heavily and Stephen was only wearing a thin jacket. When my father saw Stephen he offered him an old mac, which he no longer wore. We soon discovered why this was the case when he emerged from the house, clutching it in his hand. It was made of an iridescent material, which turned from brown to purple, the sort of mac a sixty-year-old might wear, but not a twenty-year-old. Stephen, though, didn't have the heart to tell my father that he didn't like the look of it, so he reluctantly accepted it and put it on. Once the car had rounded the corner, though, he immediately took it off and despite the foul weather, refused to wear it that day.

Stephen later told me that he actually kept the mac after he moved to London in case my father asked for it back. He stored it in a cardboard box on top of a wardrobe. Eventually, after a number of years, he threw it in the dustbin. If you ask me, that was the best place for it!

During this period, when we travelled by car with Clare and Malcolm, it wasn't long before we discovered their true nature. For example, Malcolm, Clare, Stephen, Ian and I travelled to Derby's old Baseball Ground in March 1986 and were charged seven pounds each. Even today the round trip from Darlington to Derby by car would only cost about £25, and you have to bear in mind that I'm talking about more than fourteen years ago, when the price of petrol was considerably cheaper than it is now. Naturally, we didn't mind them making a few quid for wear and tear, but to overcharge your so-called friends was despicable. I suppose we were mad for letting them get away with it for as long as we did.

At least the performance gave us something to cheer about – Quakers' well-organised defence of John Green and Peter Robinson managed to tame the potent Derby strike force of Bobby Davison and Trevor Christie for most of the game, although the latter did score after twenty-five minutes. Green was eventually led from the field and substituted on fifty-nine minutes after a clash of heads with Bobby Davison. A minute later Carl Airey touched on a free kick to Paul Ward who hammered it into the net to give us a creditable 1-1 draw. Steve Tupling was bizarrely sent off in the third minute of injury time for retaliation against John Gregory, who would later become manager of Aston Villa.

The following season Ian and I continued to travel with Clare and Malcolm. Every fortnight we'd whinge about being overcharged, but neither of us had the balls to do anything about it. Stephen also went to most of the away games, but he would make his own way there, having moved to London in May 1986. When he left Darlington it would have been easy for Stephen not to have kept in touch with me, but that's not the case at all. If anything, our friendship has grown even stronger.

Our first match of the 1986-87 season was away at York City. I went there on the train with Ian, Clare and Malcolm. Stephen travelled up from London and met us at the station for a game in which David Currie and Mark Hine were making their debuts.

Derek Hood scored first for the Minstermen from the penalty spot in the 17th minute after Phil Lloyd was adjudged to have handled the ball. However, when Tony Canham scored their second goal on the stroke of half-time he appeared to be yards offside. The lineman never raised his flag even after I shouted at him, so I turned my attention instead to Viv Busby, the York City coach, who by that time was jumping up and down celebrating the goal. But he was adamant that it was onside and ignored my protests. Incidentally, in the post-match press conference Denis Smith, the York City manager, admitted that the goal was offside, after all!

Tony Ford added a third for York on fifty-five minutes before David Currie scored a consolation goal eleven minutes from time.[2] Despite this inauspicious start, Ian and I ended up going to every match that season, both home and away.

On my twenty-second birthday in March 1987 Darlington were due to play away at Swindon. There were four of us in the car: Clare, Malcolm, Ian and me. On our way to the match, the car broke down and we ended up being stuck in Stroud for some time. Malcolm got out and telephoned the AA from a nearby garage and we began a long wait of several hours until a patrolman arrived. As we sat in the car, listening to the radio, we heard with some relief that the game had been called off because of an icy pitch.

We didn't actually know it at the time, but there was a pub within walking distance of the car! In fact, it was clearly visible over the road. Can you imagine that! I was gutted. What made this even more galling was that at five minutes past three Malcolm commented, 'Oh, look, there's a pub over there!' In other words, he waited until he knew the place would be shut before making his remark. I'm sure he did that on purpose.

At the end of March 1987 I went with Ian, Clare and Malcolm to stay with Bev and Rod in Eastleigh for the weekend. Stephen came up by train from

[2]Marco Gabbiadini was on the substitutes' bench that day for the home side. The former £1.8 million player signed for Darlington on a free transfer from York City in July 1998.

London. When we got to the house Rod offered to cook us some food. He made some sausage and bacon sandwiches and offered them round. After we all had one each he asked if anyone wanted any more. I said I'd had enough, as did Ian, but Clare and Malcolm scoffed the lot.

In the morning before we went to the match we played three-card brag. It was some time before we realised that Clare and Malcolm were cheating – they were looking at each other's hands and throwing in the weakest. But by then we'd all lost a heap of money to them. Anyway, we decided to go to the Supporters' Club bar before the match and everyone bought a round of drinks. But when it came to Clare and Malcolm's turn they got up and made straight for the door!

Bournemouth were top of the table and we were third from bottom, so you couldn't really fancy our chances that day. This was also the first game in charge for Paul Ward, who, at the age of only twenty-three, became the youngest ever manager in the Football League, a record that still stands today.

We never got to grips with the bumpy pitch and the gusty south coast wind. After the match (a predictable 1-0 defeat courtesy of a first half Mark Hine own-goal) Ian left to stay with members of his family in the Dorset area. Rod then happened to mention that he had some spare tickets for a medieval night at a pub in Bath. The tickets were only a tenner each and included not only the coach fare but also the cost of the meal, so I decided to go with them to the banquet. However, rather than joining us, Clare and Malcolm sat in Rod's house watching television. In fact, Bev got the distinct impression the following morning that they had made love that night, possibly for the first time.

In April 1987 my friend John Gray and I decided to hire a Ford Sierra to go to Swindon for the rearranged midweek fixture. Unfortunately, the two other people who were supposed to be sharing the cost of the car-hire cancelled at the last minute, which meant that the two of us had to shell out nearly £60 each. Not only that, we missed the kick-off because John decided to stop off at a well-known fish and chip shop called the Wetherby Whaler for something to eat!

This was a game when the Darlington defenders were under constant pressure, and it came as no real surprise when Bryan Wade scored for the home side after ninety minutes. Phil Lloyd tried desperately to clear the ball, but after consulting with his linesman the referee awarded the goal. Even though we lost the game 1-0, we played some excellent football, with our goalkeeper Jeremy Roberts and the defensive partnership of Gary Hinchley and Phil Lloyd particularly outstanding.

It was the return journey that proved to be so memorable. When we stopped at a pub John inadvertently locked the keys in the car, so we had to get a bloke who was drinking in the pub to open the door with a bent coathanger, and it took him ages.

On the way back, John was feeling tired so we stopped for a rest at a service station. He was having a nap while I read the Swindon programme and listened to the radio. We were just sitting in the car when all of a sudden, out of the blackness, two police cars surrounded us with blue lights flashing. It was like something out of *The Bill*. For some reason they thought we were car thieves and they therefore ordered us both to get out. I explained that I was disabled. They were still a bit dubious even when John opened the boot and showed them the wheelchair, but eventually they let us go.

Inevitably, my friendship with Clare and Malcolm ended on an acrimonious note. They knew that I had a one hundred per cent record with two away games left to play. We were due to go to Port Vale on the Saturday. I got a phone call around midnight on Friday from Clare, saying that they couldn't afford to go. I therefore rang John who said I could go on the train with him and another lad called Richard Jones.

Ian had family living in the Stoke area so I met up with him outside Vale Park. However, to my surprise when we got there we saw Clare and Malcolm's car just coming into view. Their faces drained when they saw me and to rub salt into the wound I could see that there were other people with them in the car. I was furious. I'd gone with them for almost the entire season and paid over the top prices and then they did that to me.

The Quakers hadn't registered a victory away from home all season and time was running out. Andy Jones scored first for Vale on thirty-one minutes then Alan Roberts headed in an equaliser ten minutes later. In the second half Alex Williams couldn't hold a stinging Roberts drive and Stephen Bell tapped in the rebound on sixty-five minutes. So when we won that day you can imagine the celebrations inside Vale Park.

The way that I'd been treated left a bitter taste in my mouth, so the following day I rang Clare to demand an explanation and also an apology. She claimed that she'd rung me on Saturday morning to inform me of her change of plan, but that I'd already left. When I asked my mother if there'd been a phone call for me that day she said definitely not. I then asked Clare, somewhat sarcastically, 'Did you suddenly find some money between midnight and eight in the morning?' She couldn't answer me. Her claim that they decided to go to the game at the last minute was absolute rubbish as far as I was concerned.

Nevertheless, Ian and I agreed to go with them to the last away game of the season at Chesterfield. I went under protest. I was so annoyed that I didn't even speak to them. The atmosphere in the car was frosty, to say the least. We were glad to leave them to their own devices when we arrived at Saltergate. Once again, they charged seven pounds each and there were five of us in the car. But that's only half the story.

One of the players or a club official had given them a wad of complimentary tickets. Rather than hand them out to the Darlington fans, they took theirs out and then, to my amazement, proceeded to rip up the rest. Malcolm simply threw the shredded pieces of paper on the pavement. 'I can't be arsed waiting about to give these away' was his justification. I piped up, 'Ian and I would have liked a couple of those tickets, Malcolm.' To which he replied, 'I'm sorry, I didn't think.' Ian and I just shook our heads in disbelief and vowed never to go with them again.

To add to our woes Tony Coyle drilled a right foot shot from the edge of the area low into the bottom corner after just two minutes. It was the only goal of the game. The only noteworthy event from my point of view was that Dale Anderson, a sixteen-year-old trainee, became the youngest ever player to represent Darlington, a record that still stands today.

On the way back, Ian and I never said a word. As we pulled into Darlington town centre Malcolm asked if we wanted to come with them next season. 'No thanks, we'll make alternative arrangements,' I said. A week later we lost at home against Walsall to end the season second from bottom and were relegated to the Fourth Division.

Chapter 6

As another football season drew to a close, during the summer of 1987 Stephen and I stayed for a week with our mutual friends Bev and Rod on the South Coast. While we were there Rod took Stephen and me on a visit to the Dell to see Southampton's ground for the first time. We also went on a day-trip to the Isle of Wight. While I was getting off the train one of my shoes fell underneath the coach. Fortunately, the guard managed to retrieve it from the track with a hooked pole, which meant that the train's departure time wasn't seriously delayed. Another embarrassing moment occurred on the way back to Eastleigh. To relieve the monotony of the return journey, Stephen picked up a box of matches, held it to his ear, shook it and said aloud, 'Seventeen.' Rod picked it up, rattled it and said, 'Twenty-one.' So I picked it up, but instead of shaking the *box* I shook my *head* and proclaimed, 'Nineteen!'

It was also during that holiday I decided to do something different with my life. I loved my job with Darlington FC Supporters' Club very much, but the years had moved on. I therefore decided to see the DRO (Disability Resettlement Officer) at my local Job Centre, and he advised me to go for an assessment to Preston Rehabilitation Centre, which catered specifically for the training and employment needs of disabled people.

My mother and sister were both naturally pleased when I told them what the DRO had suggested in the interview. I knew it meant a lot to my mother that I'd kept the promise I'd made to her all those years ago when I left Percy Hedley. My friends also gave me plenty of encouragement. However, rather than supporting me, my father said I was wasting my time because no one would employ me. As a matter of fact he was the one who'd said that I'd never be able to talk properly, which I did. He also said that I'd never be able to sit up unaided, which I did, so I was determined to prove him wrong once again.

Before the course started I went on the train with Ian to see Darlington's first fixture of the 1987-88 season under David Booth, which was away at Halifax Town.

When we arrived at York station we got off and waited for our connecting service to Halifax, and it was just our wretched luck that a stinking old tramp boarded the train after us with one of those shopping trolleys that seem to be the preserve of old age pensioners. His was the dirtiest, smelliest shopping trolley I'd ever seen, and rather than move it around me he proceeded to put it right over my legs. Then, catching sight of me, he said,

'What the hell have you done to yourself? You must be a freak of nature, boy.' Given his own grotesque appearance, the irony of this remark seemed to have escaped him entirely. Ian though, thought his comment hilarious and called me a freak of nature for months afterwards. In fact I think he called me that for the rest of the season.

Stephen came up from London and met us at the Shay. The game itself finished a 2-2 draw with Garry MacDonald and David Currie getting our goals, Halifax scoring their equaliser a minute before full-time.

As you'll have gathered by now, for longer journeys I prefer to travel by train, and in general my experiences of the railway system in this country have been favourable. Given my personal circumstances, since its introduction I've always had a disabled person's railcard, which entitles me to a third off the fare. These days, if you book your ticket in advance you can reserve a place for the wheelchair. Years ago, though, I used to have to travel to away games in the guard's van, cooped up behind chickenwire. Someone once said to me that if you travel the entire journey in the guard's van you can get half your money back. Well, if that's the case BR must owe me a fortune!

My six-week course at Preston Rehabilitation Centre, between August and September 1987, was a revelation. The only drawback as I saw it was the fact that, due to the nature of the place, there was a high turnover of people, so you never really got a chance to know anyone properly – in a sense, it was like a conveyor belt.

While I was at Preston I met people who had far greater problems than me, and I also got to know some nice women as well, especially a girl called Sue from Shrewsbury.[1] Every other weekend my mother and father came to collect me by car. After the assessment was over I was advised to go to Finchale Training College in Durham and they put my name down since there was a one-year waiting list.

Going to watch the Quakers – at whatever level – still held the usual fascination for me. Whether the competition was called the Associate Members Cup, the Sherpa Van Trophy or the Auto Windscreens Shield didn't concern me in the slightest. All that mattered to me was that the Quakers were involved. So, in October 1987 I went to York with Ian by car for a Freight Rover Trophy tie.

Unable to join the away supporters in the Grosvenor Road end, we were dismayed to find ourselves in the disabled area at the front of the Main

[1]Coincidentally, in February 1999, when Darlington played at Gay Meadow I bumped into Sue in Shrewsbury town centre.

Stand, beside an absolute prat of a York City fan. Since I can be one of the most opinionated and obnoxious persons alive – that's one of my biggest faults – Ian warned me, 'For God's sake, Paul, just ignore him,' so I said I'd be on my best behaviour. But this lad went droning on and on about his knowledge of football and the offside law in particular, and he was just talking bollocks as far as the two of us were concerned, so in the end, unable to bear it any longer, Ian turned to him and said, 'Shut the fuck up!'

The Barnsley manager, Allan Clarke, was watching David Currie[2] that day in what turned out to be a highly-charged derby match. Mills opened the scoring for the Minstermen on eighteen minutes, then Currie equalised on twenty-five. Peter Robinson then scored on thirty-eight minutes only for Dale Banton to equalise on fifty-three. Paul Ward added a third for the Quakers on fifty-four, but then our keeper, Paul Crichton, limped off to be replaced by Phil Bonnyman in goal. Whitehead levelled for York on sixty-nine minutes and MacDonald eventually got the winner on eighty-one.

Emotions were certainly running high during that game, so much so that David Booth was called out of the dugout by the referee, Ken Redfern, and warned that if he repeated any of his more colourful remarks he'd have to sit in the stand. Interestingly, centre half Steve Tutill, who now plays for the Quakers, was a makeshift centre-forward that day for the Minstermen.

Darlington played away at Scunthorpe on Boxing Day 1987. Ian and I travelled there in a transit van, with me sitting beside the driver. We arrived in town for opening time, and when Ian pushed my wheelchair into a pub I noticed straight away that the barmaid was ugly. I mean, *really* ugly! I remember both of us commenting on the fact. Anyway, the more we drank the better looking she became! By the end of the session we were fighting over who should buy her drinks, even asking her to confirm who had bought the last round, so eager were we to get her yet another orange juice to add to her collection!

At ten to three we were both wrecked out of our skulls as we entered the away end of the now demolished Old Show Ground. Given our bleary-eyed demeanour, we were hardly in a fit state to marvel at the imposing glass and steel architecture of the club's East Stand. This strikingly modern design was actually opened in 1958 and was the first cantilever football stand in the country. I'm surprised they even let us in the stadium, but as we entered I remember Ian commenting, 'I'm sure there's a step around here somewhere, we nearly tripped over it last yeaaargh...' Bang! He couldn't

[2]Currie was transferred to Barnsley at the end of February 1988 for £150,000. After we sold him the goals dried up and our form slumped alarmingly. Having been in contention for a play-off place, we finished the season a disappointing thirteenth in the league.

have timed it better – I was catapulted out of my chair. A steward and a policeman rushed the two of us round to the St John Ambulance first aid post. The policeman asked Ian, 'Have you been drinking?' Ian, who was virtually holding on to my wheelchair for support, said, 'No, I haven't touched a drop, Officer.' I'll never forget that reply. Naturally, I don't remember much about the game itself, except that we lost 1-0 with a goal from Andy Flounders on seven minutes.

During the course of my travels I've been unseated from my perch on a number of occasions. At Hartlepool I suffered the indignity of a broken hand, and on another occasion fell headlong down an escalator in a London tube station, sustaining nothing more serious than a cut lip. I'm certainly a living advert for seatbelt manufacturers. It's a pity that they don't fit seatbelts to wheelchairs!

In October 1988 the Quakers played Scarborough away and since we had to change at York, we decided to go for a few pints in the city. My travelling companions that day were Ian, Phil and two lads from Sheffield called Brian Elsey and Trevor Rutter, who are both originally from the Darlington area.

A week before I'd been talking about the song 'Billy, Don't Be a Hero' by the group Paper Lace. Coincidentally, the song was playing on the pub jukebox. So for a laugh the lads bound me hand and foot to the wheelchair with their scarves and made me sing it word for word before they would untie me. I wouldn't care, I don't even like the song, but fortunately I managed to remember all the words.

That day we had so many injuries that one of our forwards, Garry MacDonald, had to play in defence. Craig Short scored after twenty-one minutes for the home side and Steve Norris added a second on thirty-five. Mark Hine then hit a twenty-yard drive that went in off the underside of the crossbar to pull a goal back for the Quakers and Paul Emson scored an equaliser with a low shot from fifteen yards on seventy-six minutes. But with only six minutes remaining Norris got Scarborough's winner. Ominously, we had yet to register our first league win of the season, whereas Scarborough went top after their victory and were promoted the following year.

On the 25th of November 1988 I went with Ian to Layer Road, Colchester. We travelled to Essex on the supporters' coach, setting off at about nine in the morning. When we arrived at the ground we went to their Supporters' Club bar, which was at the top of a flight of stairs. Ian and some other lads lifted me up in my wheelchair.

From a window you could see out over the pitch. I said to Ian, 'You know, this game is never going to go ahead.' I could tell that the thick fog rolling in from the North Sea was going to make visibility very difficult for the sparse crowd of only 1,550. Despite my misgivings, the referee gave the go ahead only half an hour before kick-off.

Inside the ground we met up with Stephen, and if I remember rightly John Gray and Richard Jones were also at that game. A steward told us that the referee was insisting that it was no good having fans behind any of the goals due to the poor visibility. Instead, everyone was moved to the Main Stand, so Ian carried me up to one of the wooden bench seats.

Even from my elevated vantage point I couldn't see either set of goalposts because of the dense fog. Gary Worthington, nephew of the more famous Frank, scored a penalty for the Quakers after twenty-five minutes, then added a second after sixty-three, and Radford scored for Colchester on seventy-two. After the game I spoke to Phil Bonnyman who was naturally pleased with the result. This was the Quakers second successive away win, which hauled them off the bottom of the table. We then had a few celebratory drinks in Colchester before we caught a train back to London, since we'd arranged to stay at Stephen's house for the weekend.

The following day we thought it would be nice to watch another game in the capital so we ended up going to Upton Park, hoping to see West Ham against Everton, only to be told by a steward that there were no facilities for disabled people and that I wouldn't be allowed in because I hadn't booked four weeks in advance. I offered to pay for a seat and explained that my friends would carry me in, but I was refused admission on safety grounds. When we asked to see someone in authority, we got the same answer. This was clearly an example of blatant discrimination, so when I got home I wrote a letter of complaint to the West Ham manager, John Lyall, who offered me some free tickets, which I promptly declined.

As a footnote to the above, we went to a nearby pub in the East End for a drink. While we were sitting in the bar free sausages, sandwiches, roast potatoes and other snacks were handed round, but none were offered to us. I wasn't bothered about the food, as far as I was concerned they could shove it up their arse. The fact was that they didn't even have the decency to offer us any of their grub. So, when one of them asked us if we had a newspaper we said no. We actually had three newspapers between us, but rather than let the regulars have them we took them to the gents, flushed them down the toilet and blocked it up. So much for East End hospitality.

A few weeks later the BBC broadcast a television programme called *One in Four*. It featured a lad in a wheelchair trying to get into Upton Park. He met with the same response as I had, and I was annoyed to see the same steward who had refused me entry bar him from the ground. I rang up the BBC to explain that I'd had the same problem. Not only that, there was a double-page spread in one of the tabloids which featured another similar story. In no time at all West Ham were absolutely slaughtered for their treatment of disabled fans by the national press and television. Well-deserved criticism, if you ask me.

My trips to London with Ian when Stephen was living in Edmonton and Walthamstow seem to have generated their fair share of comical exploits.

One weekend Ian and I were staying at Stephen's flat in Edmonton. At the time he was living with his sister and her boyfriend. We'd been out on the beer again, just for a change, and when we returned to the flat Stephen decided to cook some fried eggs. He proceeded to put margarine in the pan, which put me off straight away, and he was so inebriated that he missed the pan completely when he cracked the eggs and they dropped on the kitchen floor, which, I have to say, was rather dirty.

Rather than throw them away in the bin, he scraped them up with his bare hands and put them back in the pan together with the fluff, dust, bits of eggshell and other rubbish off the floor. I said that there was no way I could even look at them, let alone eat them, and so I declined the offer, which I think was sensible. Ian, however, was so hungry that he wolfed them down, but within a minute he ran off to the toilet and was sick.

I remember an amusing encounter that took place when Stephen was living in Walthamstow. Having caught sight of my folded wheelchair outside the door of his flat, Stephen's foreign landlord asked him, in all seriousness, 'Have you bought yourself a bike?' to which Stephen replied, tongue in cheek, 'That's right – would you like a go?' Fortunately, the man didn't take Stephen up on his offer.

Perhaps the strangest series of events occurred one night when we entered a pub in Walthamstow where an elderly, pint-sized Scotsman, who claimed to have played football for AC Milan and to have known John Charles when he was at Juventus, insisted on giving me his filthy, smelly old shirt. I held it at arm's length and when we found a seat I quickly stuffed it underneath the table.

My embarrassment was further compounded by the unwanted attentions of an old woman who must have felt sorry for me. She proceeded to ask Ian in a low voice, 'How did he get to be like that?' to which Ian replied, 'Well, you know how it is when a young boy runs out in the middle of the road to fetch his ball and then gets knocked down by a car.' 'Oh, what a shame,' said the old woman, nodding her head in my direction. 'Yes,' continued Ian in surreal fashion, 'And he was nineteen years old when it happened!'

It was karaoke night at the pub, and a very young Elvis Presley impersonator was performing on stage. He must only have been in his late teens and was definitely the worst Elvis impersonator I've ever seen. He took himself really seriously, encouraged no doubt by the vocal support of the regulars who were applauding and cheering his every move. He clearly thought that they were being genuine in their enthusiasm, when they were obviously making fun of him. Some girls even cried out hysterically so he flung his scarf theatrically into the audience. This gesture was swiftly followed by us throwing the old man's shirt (the so-called AC Milan shirt, no less!) on to the stage where it hit Elvis squarely in the face.

We were all really drunk by this time, and after the young man had finished his act Stephen invited him over to our table. Elvis seemed initially quite nervous, but he eventually overcame his fear of this rather raucous section of the audience and sat down in our midst. Stephen put his arm round him in a friendly manner and asked him where he came from. Elvis replied that he was from Hackney. Stephen retorted, 'Do you mean to tell me that you've come all this way just to make a cunt of yourself?'

Chapter 7

In January 1989 my mother and I reached a momentous decision. We planned to leave my father and move to a council flat, making all the arrangements behind his back. He was actually celebrating his birthday at Hopetown and Whessoe Working Men's Club on the day we left him. We hired a removal van, took a few items of furniture and buggered off, which I thought was an excellent decision at the time. I must admit that it did cross my mind to strip the house bare, but now I'm glad that we didn't.

In my opinion he got what he deserved. Even though I'd managed, through sheer hard work, to rise above my physical limitations and was about to embark upon a college course, I felt he still refused to treat me as an equal. At one time I wanted him to be proud of my achievements, but by then I knew he would never change.

The ground floor flat in the Springfield area of Darlington was an awful mess. I was appalled when we saw it for the first time. When we decorated the place later we uncovered sixteen layers of wallpaper before we reached bare plaster. We talked long and hard about whether we should take it, but in the end we thought it could be spruced up with a little effort. Fortunately, one of my stepsisters volunteered to help us with the cleaning and the wallpaper hanging, so that by the time we moved in it was habitable.

While the property was still owned by the Council they installed a floor shower in the bathroom, and outside the flat they erected a handrail and laid some concrete paving slabs to make a ramp for my wheelchair.

This was certainly a hectic period for me because we moved on a Friday and I started my Business Studies course the following Monday at Finchale Training College. Although we left my father a note to say that we'd gone and didn't leave him a forwarding address, he still managed to find out where we were living. He came round the following Sunday, took me to one side in my bedroom and begged me to go back with him because he was lonely. I steadfastly refused and so he left, without even speaking to my mother.

Since I could hardly ask my father to take me to Finchale College in his car, my mother took me to the train station on Monday morning and when I arrived at Durham a minibus from the college was waiting to collect me. I was also lucky that a lad called David Parker from Northallerton, who was studying for an accounts course at the college, helped me out. As time went by I took more and more belongings with me to Durham, including a kettle and a portable black and white television. Not only did David offer to take me to Durham with some of my stuff, he also gave me a lift back home on

Friday and picked me up for the return journey on Sunday evening.

During this period my mother worked part-time in the evening as an office cleaner for a firm of solicitors called Close Thornton in Darlington while I studied in Durham during the week. We were both very happy doing our own thing. I came home from college on Friday night and went to the football at the weekend with my mates. My mother had her own circle of friends with whom she loved to go to the bingo, and that was fine by me. It worked out well for both of us. If I wanted to go to a nightclub it was never a problem, and if I wanted to bring a woman back home I did. My mother never stopped me from doing anything. I'll never forget her for that. She treated me like any normal twenty-three-year old.

My first impressions of Finchale College and its surroundings were distinctly favourable. It was set in its own ample tree-lined grounds, which were very pleasant indeed, and like Percy Hedley before it, catered solely for students with a disability. There were three main departments: one that taught clock and watch repair; another that offered instruction in horticulture; and last, but not least, business studies. It was in the latter department that I followed a course in secretarial studies.

Having already sampled residential life at Percy Hedley and Preston Rehabilitation Centre, I soon settled in. The facilities at Finchale College were quite adequate. My room had a bed, a wardrobe and a sink. There was a coffee vending machine in one of the corridors and a laundry on site, but I took my dirty washing home at the weekend. In my opinion, though, the food was poor. Although there was always a wide selection on the menu, as my friend Colin used to say, it was good food spoilt. There was also a refectory and a bar that opened between 6.30pm and 11pm, but I went out most nights anyway.

On Wednesday evenings a video was shown. But what annoyed me was that the college tended to be rather inflexible when it came to the imposition of what I took to be petty rules. For example, the television in the communal lounge was religiously turned off at eleven o'clock, meaning that on numerous occasions people watching a programme that didn't finish until a quarter past the hour would miss the end. Luckily, this didn't affect me personally because I had my own television from about the third or fourth week.

At first I had to share a room with a lad called Mark. As at Percy Hedley, this didn't work out in practice, through no fault of our own. In fact, we were the only two students who shared, but after two or three months I got my own room, which was much better.

College life was certainly eventful and exciting. I can remember that on my twenty-fourth birthday my classmates got me a strippergram. The girl took most of my clothes off, which shocked me quite a bit, but then she took most of hers off as well, so that made it all worthwhile! After that we went down town and I got absolutely rat-arsed. How the hell I got up in the morning I'll never know.

My feelings of exhilaration, however, were soon put into perspective after the Quakers sunk to a new low in even their history. That season the team was sponsored by a local company, Industrial Scaffolding Limited, but no amount of shoring-up could help us.

The penultimate game was away to Scunthorpe United on the 6th of May, and we desperately needed to win to avoid relegation. Ian picked me up in his car at about ten in the morning. For once, he was actually on time! We were both quite optimistic about our chances of surviving the drop and saw plenty of fans in cars and coaches making the same journey as us. We arrived at about midday and parked in the car park of the Berkeley pub near the ground. We then went for a drink where we mingled with the home and away fans.

Ian pushed me the short distance to the ground and we paid our entrance money. We both shelled out sixty pence each for a programme and Ian lifted me out of my wheelchair and into one of the seats of the Caparo Stand. This was my first ever visit to Scunthorpe's new Glanford Park stadium, its breezeblock and corrugated iron structure more reminiscent of a cattle market than a football ground. However, there were so many fans packed in the away end that I could hardly see the game with all the bodies in front of me. 'The Darlo's stayin' up, the Darlo's stayin' up. Now are you gonna believe us, now are you gonna believe us, now are you gonna believe us, the Darlo's stayin' up!' The seven hundred or so supporters behind me kept up this chant for most of the first half.

By half-time we were already 1-0 down, though it certainly wasn't a case of one-way traffic. For example, Scunthorpe's goalkeeper, Paul Musselwhite, was fortunate to tip a Garry MacDonald header on to his post. But after a twelve minute spell in the second half we were 5-0 down, with Tony Daws scoring a hat trick. The only bright spot was Paul Willis's magnificent eightieth minute consolation goal from all of thirty yards.

The final scoreline was 5-1, which ensured that we were relegated to the Vauxhall Conference. Brian Little, who would later become one of our most successful postwar managers, had taken over from David Booth in February, but the team was very poor and he was on a hiding to nothing.

Ironically, David Cork, who would later sign for us and spearhead our push for promotion, played for the Iron that day.

I'll certainly never forget the emotion after the game – Ian and I were in tears along with many other grown men and women. Yet, despite having suffered such a crushing defeat, the fans shouted for the team to come back out on the field, which they did. Our centre-forward, Garry MacDonald, came over to apologise in person and threw his shirt into the crowd. Even the Scunthorpe fans commiserated with us and sang in comradely fashion, 'You'll be back...*You'll* be back'

But it was what happened afterwards that stood out. On the way back from the game Ian and I were silent, lost in our own thoughts. We didn't speak the whole journey. It was like having suffered a bereavement. In fact, Ian seemed to be driving in a trance. Anyway, we made it back to Colburn from Scunthorpe in just under an hour and a quarter. We arrived at his local pub, the Colburn Lodge, at about a quarter past six, but nobody would believe that we'd been to the match. They all thought we were lying. So as proof we showed them our programmes.

Several weeks before the traumatic events at Scunthorpe, I met a woman called Louise, purely as the result of an accident. I was enjoying a night out with friends in a club in Durham called the Cueball. She was carrying a tray of drinks to her table when she tripped over my wheelchair. At first she looked annoyed, but then our eyes met and she smiled. She left all the broken glasses on the floor, sat down and started chatting. After the nightclub had closed she invited me back to her place. I couldn't take her back to Finchale since one of the college rules was that no women were allowed in students' rooms. We talked for ages. She told me that her husband was in the army and that she was unhappy. I told her everything about my life, including my struggles to get on in the world and my family circumstances.

Before I knew it, it was eight o'clock in the morning. I had to be at college for eight thirty so I hurriedly left and promised to see her the following Sunday. Luckily, my friend Colin had signed me out for the night, otherwise I would have been in serious trouble when my carer arrived in the morning to find that my bed hadn't been slept in.

When I got back to college the lads asked me what had happened. They just didn't believe me when I said that we'd talked all night. I went back to Louise's on Sunday. Once again we talked, but this time we ended up going to bed and making love over and over again to a song by Queen entitled, appropriately enough, 'I Want it All.'

Although Louise was great fun to be with she certainly wasn't a very houseproud person. Colin would often drop me off in a taxi and say to me, 'I'm not going in there.' But she was very caring and would do absolutely anything for me; for example, she persuaded her brother to drive us to the Darlington player of the year award, which was held in the town's Cricket Club.

So, there I was, working hard at Finchale College during the daytime, sleeping with Louise at night and then returning at six o'clock in the morning. Although I liked Louise very much we were never in love; it was more of a mutual need. In many ways, I think I used her for sex. As the reader will discover later in the book, she wasn't the only married woman I've been involved with and I suppose she won't be the last. We certainly got on well and I went out with her for a full year.

However, our relationship did affect my coursework to an extent, because I was naturally worn out after spending so many long nights with her. Fortunately, my typing tutor, Maureen Summers, was very perceptive and worked out what was happening. One day she took me to one side and said, 'Paul, if you don't slow down a bit and sort yourself out you're going to blow everything.' That certainly made me think. And it was the way she said it. She didn't tell me not to see Louise, she just pointed out that my grades were going down and advised me to reconsider my priorities. That really made me wake up to my responsibilities.

Although I didn't finish with Louise as such I saw much less of her and put more effort into my studies. As a matter of fact, we kept in touch by letter even after the course had finished, although we did eventually go our separate ways. I'm convinced that if it hadn't have been for Maureen Summers I would never have passed the course and got a job later on. I've got a lot to thank her for. I would certainly recommend Finchale College to anyone in a similar position as myself. As a thank you, in July 1989, I completed the Great North Run in my wheelchair and handed the principal of the college a cheque for £256.

Those were certainly the best days of my life on a social level. We used to get a bus to Durham from the college every Thursday night and would go on a pub crawl. Our favourite pubs in the city were the Market Tavern, the Hogshead, the Fighting Cocks and the Angel. My friend Colin who came from Redcar always used to sign me out so that I didn't get into any trouble.

We were a group of likeminded disabled people, who each had problems one way or the other and got on well together. There was Jason from Bradford, who like Colin had lost a leg in a car accident, Big Ian from

Newcastle, who had a back injury, and a guy called Richard, who hailed from the South Coast. Some of the things we used to get up to don't bear thinking about.

Once I was at the bus stop, smoking some wacky baccy, when a teacher from the college came into view. Instead of stubbing out the joint, I foolishly swallowed it while it was still alight. On another occasion I was so stoned that I circled a red litter-bin in my wheelchair, whooping and chanting, because I genuinely thought it was a camp fire and that I was an American Indian!

Another time I'd left the plastic bottle behind in my room that I use when I need to urinate. Obviously, being in a wheelchair means that I can't stand up at a urinal, so instead I pee in a plastic bottle and empty it down the toilet. Since I needed to go rather urgently, instead of making for the toilet down the corridor, I decided to do it in my room and empty the bottle down the sink. Colin was with me at the time and saw a cleaner walking past the door, which was slightly ajar. So he shouted, 'Hey, missus, come and have a look at this!' The cleaner walked in and saw me with the bottle in my hand and my trousers round my ankles. When she saw what I was doing she exclaimed, 'That is absolutely disgusting' and burst into tears. Not surprisingly, she reported our behaviour to Maureen Summers who, to our great relief, laughed the incident off as an innocent prank. The cleaner, however, never forgot what had happened and from that moment onwards ignored us. Every time I passed her in the corridor I couldn't help smirking just a little bit!

One night Colin and I returned to the college at half past twelve after a session on the booze. Unfortunately, a big bald security guard intercepted us and proceeded to rebuke me. As he was leaning over me and pointing out the error of my ways I could see Colin slowly unzipping his flies and taking his dick out. Unknown to the security guard, Colin pretended to slap him over the head with it like a fish and the man didn't even notice!

After yet another boozy Thursday night out in Durham I stayed at Louise's and only returned to the college at a quarter to nine. Colin was sitting in the hallway. Normally he'd have been in lessons by then so I asked him what he was doing there. 'I've just got up' was his innocent reply. Then he continued, 'Shall we push off?' I nodded and went to fetch my holdall and we left. I was back home after ten in the morning. My mother, who was naturally quite surprised to see me, looked me in the eye and asked, 'Paul, are you skiving?' I couldn't lie, and admitted that I was, to which she said matter of factly, 'That's all I want to know' and left it at that.

I can remember one of our tutors saying that we were the most disruptive group of students he'd ever had. I think the lecturers wrote Fridays off, especially with our group, because they were just a waste of time. The whole class was crazy. I was lucky to fall in with such a fantastic group of people, because it could quite easily have been the other way around. I could have been stuck with a lot of boring farts instead. Yet we all managed to pass our exams. To use the well-worn cliché, we played hard but we worked hard. And that is important, because you always have to remember why you're there.

While I was at Finchale College I wrote to local companies for work placements. The first one I obtained was at Cummins Engine Company in Darlington. Here I was put under the wing of a lady called Win Crow and she taught me a lot about work practices. I enjoyed my five weeks there from October to November 1989 in the computer department. Cummins even paid me a wage of £30 a week – this was the maximum I could earn before income tax would have been deducted. My second work placement followed immediately afterwards at the Employment Service in Darlington.

To be honest, I hated it there and was glad to leave. The majority of the staff seemed to be frightened of me and hardly spoke at all, although a couple of them were pleasant enough.

Although my grades had slipped slightly, after I bucked up my ideas I came out with eight qualifications in total.[1] And for the Pitman English for Business Communications I received a First Class Pass with a mark of 90 per cent, the only student in my year to achieve such a result. So that wasn't too bad. But I also came away from Finchale College with a lot of memories that are just as important to me.

[1]RSA Numeracy Stage 1, RSA Typewriting Skills (Stages 1 & 2), RSA Computer Literacy and Information Technology, Pitman Typewriting (Elementary and Intermediate), Pitman English for Business Communications (Intermediate), and Pitman Practical Wordprocessing (Intermediate).

Chapter 8

Once I'd recovered from the seismic shock to my nervous system brought on by our relegation to the Vauxhall Conference League, life as a Darlington supporter became more bearable following our terrific start to the new season.

By the time Ian and I travelled to Cheltenham on the supporters' coach in December 1989, we were top of the table. Incidentally, we decided to travel with the Supporter's Club to some away games as most were in the midlands or the south of the country, though more often than not, we went by car or train. History was about to be made – this was the first ever meeting between Darlington and Cheltenham, as well as my first visit to their ground.

Having left Feethams at about eight in the morning, we stopped off at the Trowell service station near Nottingham before we made our way to Cheltenham, arriving at about one o'clock. When our driver pulled into a superstore car park near the Robins' Whaddon Road ground, the police ordered all the supporters to stay on board the coach. I told a white lie and said that I had to get off and empty my catheter bag. As the reader will remember, I'm not fitted with a catheter at all, I just use a plastic bottle if I need to urinate, but the police weren't to know that. So they let Ian get me off the coach and we went for four or five pints while the others stayed put. This was one of those very rare occasions when being disabled had its advantages!

The game itself was a scrappy affair, a situation that wasn't helped by the blustery wind and driving rain. Cheltenham had signed Andy Gray, the former Aston Villa striker, from Glasgow Rangers in the close season, but he limped off four minutes into the second half. His impact on the game was minimal – he did nothing but mouth off to the referee and whinge to his team-mates (ideal preparation, I would have thought, for his future role as a football pundit on Sky television!). Athough Les McJannet was harshly sent off for the Quakers after only twenty-four minutes, we scored through Paul Emson with only eight minutes of the match remaining, so it was a good day all round.

Stephen, however, just couldn't contain his excitement when we got what proved to be the winner. He easily hurdled the low perimeter fence as he attempted to sprint across the pitch and congratulate the goalscorer, but because of the heavy ground he couldn't catch our winger, so he gave up and rejoined the crowd. Fortunately, Stephen's rush of blood occurred in more enlightened times when a fan who strayed onto the pitch wasn't liable to be bundled away by stewards and banned for life.

Cheltenham Spa with its fashionable shops and listed buildings struck me as quite an unlikely hotbed of football. Although the team was sponsored by Gulf Oil, who had their headquarters in the town, the programme only reinforced that initial impression: the front cover photograph shows a fine row of elegant Regency houses and beautifully tended flowerbeds. More like Harrogate, in fact, than Hartlepool!

Three days later, I visited Runcorn. This was more like the kind of place you'd expect a football team to flourish: a northern industrial town near the Manchester Ship Canal. It was a bitterly cold December afternoon when Ian picked me up in his car after work and we made the short journey to Cheshire. We arrived at about seven o'clock with only time for a swift half before we made our way to the ramshackle Canal Street ground, which is where I bumped into my friend Steve Keeney. As we approached the turnstile, we had to negotiate what was in effect a ploughed field! Once inside the ground, before the game kicked off, Steve went to the refreshment kiosk to get a cup of tea, only to find that the queue was a mile long. Not only that, they were using a small calor gas stove underneath a ten gallon urn of ice-cold water in a vain attempt to bring it to the boil!

At half-time, with the home side 2-0 up, Steve eventually managed to get served by the old dear in the refreshment kiosk. But when he handed over a fifty pence piece for a Mars bar she was so confused that she couldn't work out the correct change.

What amazed me, though, was the state of the toilet. Mind you, one time at Rochdale I couldn't use the gents because it was inaccessible and so I had to use the ladies instead. That toilet was the dirtiest and smelliest I'd ever seen in my life. It reminded me of a scene from *Trainspotting* – you know the one I mean!

By contrast, the toilet at Runcorn was only half-built. There was simply a breezeblock wall a few courses high to shelter me from the brass-monkey weather and protect my modesty at the same time! I suppose I should have been grateful that I could still watch the match from my vantage point, but the result certainly wasn't to my taste either because we lost 2-1 with David Cork replying for the Quakers. Incidentally, Ian Woan, who later signed for Nottingham Forest, played in midfield for Runcorn that night.

The dilapidated state of the Canal Street ground had much in common with Barrow's bleak Holker Street, which we visited on New Year's Day. The latter was in so much of a state of disrepair that the lads had a whipround at half-time and collected £30 towards the cost of a new stand!

The race for the title was still very much in the balance in March 1990 when we played Northwich Victoria at their Drill Field ground. Northwich were one of four former league sides in the Vauxhall Conference that season if you include ourselves – the other two being Merthyr and Barrow. In fact, Northwich were founder members of Division Two in 1892, but they only lasted two seasons before they dropped out of the league in 1894, never to return. This was our third meeting that season – we had already comprehensively beaten them 4-0 in the league and 6-2 in the first round of the FA Cup.

After I'd left work, my father dropped me off in the car (for a fee!) at Catterick Bridge. Ian then drove me the rest of the way and we parked in a side street near the ground, arriving just in time for the evening kick-off.

The third encounter between the two sides, however, was a brutal affair. Northwich resorted to the most cynical tactics, which amounted to kicking our players off the pitch. There was even a rumour that the chairman of one of our promotion rivals had offered the Northwich players £1,000 per man to stop us from winning, though I should add that this rumour was never substantiated.

With only fourteen minutes on the clock, Neil Robinson had to leave the field after he was on the receiving end of a two-footed tackle, and his ankle ligament damage was so serious that he never played professional football again. On top of that, after thirty-five minutes Kevan Smith, who had rejoined the club from York City in the close season, sustained a head wound that required several stitches. As he lay on the pitch receiving treatment from our physio an old woman in the Northwich area shouted, 'I hope he's swallowed his tongue and dies.' After ten minutes of treatment Kev returned to the fray with his head swathed in bandages, but his stitches burst open during the game so the wound had to be hurriedly re-sewn. He also required further attention later for five broken teeth.

On fifty-five minutes Northwich scored. Two minutes later our goalkeeper, Mark Prudhoe, and John Stringer both went for a 50-50 ball. Prudhoe came off worst, received a nasty gash to his thigh from the opposing player's raking studs and had to be carried off on a stretcher. The tackle that caused this appalling injury was only punished with a booking, yet it kept Prudhoe out of the side for more than five weeks. He was even taken to hospital and kept in for observation. After this incident Brian Little and his opposing number, Cliff Roberts, became embroiled in a spot of gesticulating, which a linesman managed to bring under control. When the commotion had died down our centre-forward, John Borthwick, ended up in goal. It was hardly a surprise then that we lost this bruising encounter 1-0 and went second in the table to Barnet.

The final match of the season, Welling United away in May 1990, was a nail-biting affair. We set off from Darlington early on Saturday morning. There were three of us in the car that day: Ian, a lad called Graham Dixon from Bishop Auckland and myself. When we arrived in London at about midday we dropped the car off outside Stephen's house in Bounds Green and then caught a southbound train across the Thames to Welling, where we met up in a pub with Trevor Rutter, Brian Elsey and Phil Rutter (no relation to Trevor). I remember a girl we called 'Sweet Sixteen', who went to most of the away games that season, always had her eye on Trevor. To wind him up we sang, 'She's nearly sixteen' along Welling High Street, which drove him barmy!

Well over a thousand Darlington fans packed into the away end of the leafy Park View Road ground. There was a carnival mood, some supporters wearing fancy dress, such as a clown's outfit. A veteran fan called Brian even turned up sporting his kilt. To cap it all it was a scorching day, with a temperature in the eighties, the pitch was bone-hard and the away fans in the Danson Park End were exposed to the baking sun, since the ground largely consisted of open terracing.

What an unforgettable experience! We got there early and the atmosphere was brilliant. It wasn't a particularly good spectacle from a purist's point of view, but the meaning of the game was more important than the game itself.

With only three minutes remaining Paul Emson was brought down by a late tackle on the left wing. Andy Toman swung in a cross to the far side of the penalty area where substitute Gary Coatsworth rose unchallenged to send a looping header past Paul Barron. It was his first ever senior goal. I went wild. Some fans even staged a premature pitch invasion and police on horseback were needed to restore order. Certain people won't be able to understand that kind of behaviour, but if your heart is in a club you kick every ball and save every shot, as if your life depended upon it. Besides, the word 'fan' is just a shorter version of 'fanatic,' which, as my dictionary says, is someone who is 'inspired by a god, frenzied, mad.' I certainly behaved like a madman that day when we achieved promotion back to the football league under Brian Little, having been relegated the previous season.

After the game Stephen, Phil, 'Sweet Sixteen', Brian, Trevor, Ian and myself stood for a while between the posts where the winning goal had been scored and had our photographs taken. Then we sank a few pints in Welling itself – we sat in a park near the ground where Graham did celebratory handstands. People were looking out of their windows at us, probably thinking that we were crazy, maybe never having seen so many football fans before.

We caught a train back to the West End and went to several pubs. I eventually ended up in the Trafalgar Square fountain up to my arse in water with all the lads dancing around me. What a night! We caught the tube to Bounds Green, and Ian certainly caused a few raised eyebrows amongst the other passengers when he took off his shoes and started wringing out his wet socks! Some of the lads even had to dry out their soggy train tickets later with a hair dryer, which I thought was highly amusing.

After we got off the tube I remember being pushed down Whittington Road, just a few yards from Stephen's place. It was one o'clock in the morning and the Chinese takeaway was obviously closed. Not discouraged by the sign on the door, Stephen woke up the proprietor by knocking loudly and shouting, 'I want some chips' at the top of his voice. When the owner's head appeared at an upstairs window he quite understandably told us to fuck off, and then in milder terms said, 'No, no. I not serve you. We closed. You go home now.' We must have made a strange sight, still sopping-wet and bedraggled from our soaking in the Trafalgar Square fountain. But Stephen simply wouldn't take no for an answer and even shouted his order through the letterbox. In the end, just to get rid of us, the poor man cooked us all a meal, nervously handing each parcel of food through the gap in the door. Throughout this whole episode he left the door on its security-chain, because he was still too frightened to open it fully.

Returning to the large five-bedroomed terraced house, we unwrapped our food and sat down to our feast. All the other tenants were absent that day because it was the Bank Holiday weekend, so the seven of us – Stephen, Ian, Brian, Trevor, Graham, Phil and myself – stayed the night. Ian and Brian, though, ended up sharing a double bed. Despite having consumed a bellyful of beer, Ian was awake and dressed at six in the morning. 'What are you doing up at the crack of dawn?' asked a somewhat bemused Stephen, when he caught sight of him. 'Well, would *you* like to spend the night with Brian?' came Ian's sharp-witted reply!

Chapter 9

If you exclude my six-year association with Darlington FC Supporters' Club as an Order Clerk, my experiences of the world of work were somewhat limited in their scope. In September 1987, for example, I was recruited as a part-time Access Guide Officer for Darlington Association on Disability. The post entailed visiting pubs, shops and other public buildings in order to establish whether or not they were accessible for disabled people and to determine the type of facilities they provided. Although it was unpaid, I was able to claim my daily expenses. It was a job that I enjoyed very much as it enabled me to meet a lot of interesting people, and the information I collected along with the other volunteers was eventually published in a booklet.

In June 1988, having researched the Access Guide for about nine months, and just before I attended Finchale Training College, I changed jobs and went to the *Rathbone Society*[1] as a typist. This was the first position for which I received a wage. While I was there I learned the practical office skills that were essential if I was to find myself a clerical post. I did some typing, filing, photocopying and learned how to operate the switchboard. I met some nice people there, too, in particular Joanne, the supervisor.

When I left Finchale Training College in December 1989 I was determined to find myself an office job that would build on the Business Studies qualifications I had gained and allow me to achieve a certain degree of financial independence. To increase my chances of obtaining such a post, I offered my services, on a voluntary part-time basis, as a typist for Darlington Citizens' Advice Bureau from February to September 1990. I obtained the position via Darlington College of Technology Job Club. I enjoyed working there and Peter Trenouth, the centre manager, was a great help to me, especially in the provision of references to prospective employers.

I continued to go to the Job Club for six months, five days a week between nine in the morning and one o'clock in the afternoon, but I must say that most of the people there were just a waste of space. They weren't interested in looking for a job at all. They only attended because they had been unemployed for six months and had been told to go. Consequently, they would sit around reading the various newspapers or filling in the crossword instead of looking at the situations vacant. They would frequently make up excuses, saying that they were ill, so that they wouldn't have to come in at

[1]A charitable organisation that employed people on government-funded schemes.

all. I found that exceptionally frustrating. Here I was with problems of my own, genuinely trying to find a job, and there they were making paper aeroplanes out of old newspapers. It was like being back at Percy Hedley.

Quite a lot of them were hopeless cases, but the staff were really good in very difficult conditions. I'm not saying that everyone who was there at that time wasn't looking for a job, because some clearly were, but the majority were not. They were there under duress.

What made this attitude even harder to understand was that my own endeavours to gain suitable employment as a disabled person were often thwarted by discrimination. I wrote letter after letter to local firms, without any success. One day I saw a job advertised in *The Northern Echo* and when I rang the company I was invited to attend an interview. But when I mentioned that I was in a wheelchair the person on the other end of the telephone hesitated and then suddenly remembered that the job had been taken. Even when I wasn't at the Job Club I was writing letters or filling in application forms. On average, I was applying for a job every day. Three particular incidents, which all took place in 1990, stand out in relation to discrimination.

I applied for a job as a clerk/typist with a well-known supermarket in Darlington. It was a post that was well within my capabilities, and I was pleased and somewhat surprised to receive a letter asking me to attend an interview.

When I arrived the personnel officer said, 'Oh, dear, you're in a wheelchair!'

I replied, 'Yes, I mentioned it on my application form.'

She explained, 'Oh, I'm afraid we can't possibly employ someone in a wheelchair because the office is upstairs. I'll interview you anyway, but you haven't got the job.'

I said, 'Surely, you must have read my application form. Why did you invite me down here if you knew that I couldn't be employed?'

'You obviously didn't put it on your application form, young man,' was her pompous reply.

I countered, 'I'm sorry, but I did. I'll tell you what, why don't you go upstairs and get the form. You obviously haven't planned your interview very well and I shall be writing to your head office.'

Her attitude suddenly changed.

'Oh...yes...I'm really sorry.'

My response was to go on the offensive.

'I'm not at all happy with your attitude. You've basically called me a liar.

I'd like you to find my application form so that we can settle this matter once and for all.'

'There's obviously been some mistake,' she conceded at last.

I scented victory.

'You're quite right. There certainly has been a mistake. You've read through my application form, not noticing that I'm in a wheelchair, and asked me to come for an interview.'

She then went upstairs to look for my application form. It was a good fifteen minutes before she returned with the form in her hand.

'I'm really sorry. You did mention that you're in a wheelchair. It's my fault entirely. Since you're here I will interview you, but you haven't got the job.'

So I sat through an interview that meant nothing to me. After so much preparation on my part, I was shocked at the way I'd been treated. This was the first time that I'd come across such blatant discrimination. I did write later to the head office of this particular company and received a letter of apology, informing me that the personnel officer had been reprimanded for her insensitive action.

By this time, Peter Ray, who worked for *The Spastics Society*,[2] had learned of my plight from *The Northern Echo*. I'd written to the paper in April 1990 and they'd printed an article entitled 'Job hunter attacks "prejudiced" employers' about my experiences of discrimination in employment. The paper mentioned the fact that I'd applied for one hundred jobs but only been offered one interview. The accompanying photograph showed me holding a sheaf of rejection letters. Indeed, between January 1990 to September of that year I applied for a total of 203 jobs and obtained eight interviews. When Peter Ray saw the article he decided to help me get a job.

On one occasion Peter went with me to an interview in Bedale for a County Council clerical post. I'd checked in advance that there was suitable access for wheelchairs and been told that there would be no problem at all.

To my utter amazement, we were confronted with a huge, curving marble staircase. It reminded me of one I had seen in the film *Gone with the Wind*. I said, 'How the hell do you expect me to climb that?' And the reply was, 'Oh, I didn't think about getting you up the stairs, I only considered access inside the building.'

It wasn't worth trying to get me up. Even with a stair-climber,[3] it would have been dangerous. I suppose you could put this example down to stupidity rather than discrimination, but it was still annoying nonetheless.

[2]This organisation has now been renamed *SCOPE*.

[3]A portable device that can be used by disabled people to negotiate straight flights of stairs.

The manager, too embarrassed to make an appearance, sent his secretary to apologise on his behalf. I should add that I wasn't reimbursed in any way for my wasted journey.

The third example of discrimination was a job interview that I attended in Darlington. Unbeknown to the company, I knew one of the other candidates. This particular person didn't have my qualifications or experience. When she got the job I was 99.99 per cent sure that I'd lost out because I was in a wheelchair. I'd like to think that things have improved since then, but I'm not so sure.

It was about this time that I sent off a speculative letter to a company called Farmway Ltd in Darlington, and following an interview they promised to keep me in mind for any vacancies that might crop up in the future. In June Farmway got in touch with Peter Ray. They'd remembered me because they were actively seeking to employ a disabled person, so I was offered a job as full-time 'Farmwatch'[4] coordinator to start in September 1990. Although they did everything right when they appointed me, I don't think they gave sufficient thought to what the post would actually entail.

To be absolutely truthful, 'Farmwatch' was only really a part-time job, so I was bored a lot of the time. There I was, fresh from a Business Studies Course, with twelve qualifications in total under my belt, typing up internal envelopes! That was hardly a sensible state of affairs.

On a few occasions I helped type up statements for the Credit Control Department when they were busy, and I'll never forget Linda and Ruth who were two of the most supportive colleagues anyone could possibly ask for.

Their support was crucial when I had a personality clash with a senior member of staff. He was one of those people who just couldn't see past my wheelchair. Eventually, he left the company, though not before he'd provided me and the rest of the staff with two moments of pure comedy, which I feel must be set down here.

The first incident occurred when he was sent on an assignment to one of our branches, just over the border in Scotland. He'd been despatched to take photographs of JCBs or suchlike farm machinery for a glossy publication only to discover, on his return, that he'd forgotten to put a film in his camera!

The second howler occurred one day in the firm's car park. It was an exceptionally windy day and as he was getting out of his car a violent gust caught hold of his wig and dislodged it. Trying desperately to save face, he

[4]'Farmwatch' is a crime-prevention scheme for rural communities. It is similar, in many important respects, to its urban equivalent 'Neighbourhood Watch.'

caught hold of it before it blew away and attempted to restore his dignity, but only succeeded in making a bad job of putting it back on. You can imagine the stifled laughter that ensued when he entered the office with his hairpiece askew.

In moments of idleness, mischief-making was never far from my thoughts and that of my fellow employees. There was, for instance, the infamous 'paper clip prank.' My friend Stephen Luck and another man would stand at the toilet window on the second floor and fire paper clips with the aid of an elastic band at unsuspecting customers walking across the car park while I sat in my chair and received a running commentary. I can remember one occasion when a man was hit in the throat and fell to the ground like a sack of spuds. At the end of a working day the car park used to be littered with spent paper clips.

Stephen was also fond of playing practical jokes on me. Once he telephoned the local adult bookshop and gave them my extension number. When the phone rang a man at the other end asked if I'd ordered some Gay magazines. Naturally, I indignantly claimed not to know anything about it.

When a new YTS trainee started we played quite a good joke on him. You might be familiar with such initiation rituals yourself – being asked to go for a long stand, a glass magnet or a box of sparks for the grinder. The trick we played was quite original. Our victim was only sixteen and the lads got some gear from the stores for him to wear – a boiler suit, green wellies, a face mask, goggles and elbow-length rubber gloves. The intention was to get him to take me to the toilet. To add to the effect I let slip that I'd had a curry the night before so I might have a bit of diarrhoea. My friend Eddie then added, 'That's why you have to wear these gloves!' Naturally, the poor lad was mightily relieved to discover, after having pushed me into the toilet, that it was all a wind-up.

I actually did some work, too, you'll be relieved to hear in my time at Farmway! I became responsible for the distribution of internal vacancies and placing advertisements in the local and national press. I also booked spaces for the company at various agricultural shows throughout the region, raised cheques for payment and edited the monthly *Farmway Focus* newsletter. When a new personnel manager arrived he saw that I was capable of doing much more and ensured that I got a decent computer.

On the whole Farmway were good to me.[5] Not that they were out of pocket themselves. Since my office was on the second floor, I needed a stair-climber

[5] I left their employ in September 1998

to reach it, and it was the Employment Service who provided this free of charge. Later still, Farmway received a grant for the provision of a disabled toilet. They also received a grant towards the cost of buying a photocopier and a personal computer. Additionally, the government paid forty per cent of my wages.

Financially, though, I was definitely worse off than I would have been if I'd remained unemployed, but I'd rather have a job anyway. Since I was on a low wage my earnings were topped up by two benefits: DLA (Disabled Living Allowance) and DWA (Disabled Working Allowance) and my taxi fares to and from work were paid for out of my Mobility Allowance. Even so there's still very little incentive, apart from self-respect, for a disabled person to find employment and I think that has to change.

Another factor that endeared Farmway to me was that they made allowances for my football fever and let me take time off work to follow my chosen team. In my spell at Finchale Training College and my first year at Farmway the most amazing turnaround in the Quakers fortunes had been effected.

Chapter 10

During the Quakers' second promotion season Ian and I went to every game both home and away, which I suppose was quite an achievement.

Perhaps the most memorable match, for purely personal reasons, was against Maidstone United in October 1990. By the time we got to London, where we rendezvoused with Stephen, we'd been drinking all the way down on the train. My travelling companions that day were Ian and Phil, and we met up with Brian and Trevor later in a pub in Dartford.

Maidstone had actually sold their London Road ground to the MFI furniture group in 1988. Since their promotion from the Vauxhall Conference in 1989, at our expense, they were sharing Southern League Dartford's Watling Street ground while they were engaged in a planning dispute with the local council over a proposal to build a new stadium.[1]

I ended up being perched rather precariously on the terraces and said to Phil, 'Move me along a bit, mate, I can't see a bloody thing.' But rather than shove me sideways he pushed me forwards and I fell headlong down the steps and was knocked out cold. The next thing I remember was being put in an ambulance, though I must have had some of my wits about me because I apparently insisted on buying a match programme before I left for the hospital, and wouldn't budge until I got one!

Within about half an hour, despite a severe headache, my concussion had eased somewhat and I wanted to get back to the game. I explained to the nurse that I'd forked out £40 for the train fare and wasn't prepared to miss the rest of the game, so would she stitch my head wound because I wanted to leave. She, however, had other ideas and said I ought to stay in the hospital overnight as a precaution. I said, 'I don't think so' and so she stitched up my head and we hurriedly left.

Outside the hospital we collared a taxi driver and offered to pay him five pounds each if he could get us back to the ground within five minutes. He drove like a bat out of hell and I saw the last two goals that sealed our victory, so it was worth it in the end. We actually won 3-2 with goals from Cork, Borthwick and Toman.

After the game, we went to the West End to celebrate. Things were still hazy for me – I didn't feel very well, had a stinking headache, several stitches in my wound and a massive bandage round my head. To be on the safe side,

[1]As it turned out, Maidstone United never did manage to get a new stadium built, despite spending millions of pounds on planning applications. After only three seasons in the Football League, in early August 1992, just days before the first fixture of the new season, they folded and now languish six leagues below the present Third Division.

one of the lads phoned up one of my stepsisters to explain what had happened to me, and she told him not to let me fall asleep or get drunk. Fatal! I downed seven pints and fell asleep in the pub! So much for stepsisterly advice.

In February 1991 Ian and I took part in a sponsored wheelchair push from Scorton Hospital in North Yorkshire to Victoria Park, Hartlepool, for the derby match.[2] My wheelchair was even equipped with a bicycle lamp because we set off just before midnight, and that day it rained on and off so I had a plastic bin liner over my legs to keep them dry.

Coincidentally, my future fiancée, Heather, was actively involved in the preparations for our latest expedition – she volunteered to make the sandwiches and provided the refreshments. The day was marred, however, by two rather ugly incidents. When we went round the pitch before kick-off with a blanket to collect more money, someone flung a tin opener at us. Later, towards the end of the match, Heather's son was injured by a firework thrown by an irresponsible Darlington fan. On a more light-hearted note, Ian's father got his foot stuck in one of the goal nets as he accompanied us on our lap of honour!

The trip also had an inauspicious beginning. Two weeks previously my wheelchair had been stolen from the Farmway office in King Street while I was at my desk, so I had to use my oldest wheelchair in its place.

Fortunately, these incidents were all put into perspective after our meeting with the Hartlepool and former Darlington manager, the late, great Cyril Knowles, who unexpectedly joined us as we approached Victoria Park. Mind you, I was a bit concerned when he gave me a Hartlepool scarf to wear!

When Cyril drew near I could see that he didn't look well at all and even commented on the fact. He mentioned that he'd been suffering from headaches of late, to which I replied that it was probably stress. A week later, though, he was lying seriously ill in hospital, never to recover.

After my gruelling journey I was invited into the home dressing room to change my clothes, and Pop Robson helped me to get ready. Brian Honour, himself a former Darlington midfielder, handed over some more money – £60 I think it was – after the Hartlepool players had an impromptu whip-round. Altogether, we raised more than £2,000 for the Darlington Association on Disability and the Alzheimer's Disease ward at Scorton Hospital, where Ian's grandmother was a patient. The game itself was

[2]This was not the first time that I'd made this particular journey – on Boxing Day 1983 a lad called Peter Curtis pushed me to Hartlepool and we managed to raise £278 for Darlington FC. We presented the cash to the then Darlington manager, Cyril Knowles, on the Feethams pitch before our third round FA Cup tie against Maidstone United.

played on a mud bath of a pitch and Mark Prudhoe performed heroically in goal to earn us a 0-0 draw.

In April 1991 Ian and I were going to travel to Cardiff to see Darlington play, so I stayed at his house in Catterick the night before. As usual we decided to go night-clubbing. Me being me, I ended up really drunk and got fixed up with a woman. Ian said to me, 'I don't care what you do Paul but you'll have to be up at six o'clock sharp.' I replied, 'No problem. *I'll* be up by then.'

At six o'clock Ian came into the bedroom, but unfortunately I was still messing about with the woman I'd met in the nightclub. There I was, half-cut, while Ian was trying to put my shoes on! Ian's wife Lynne was quite disgusted by my behaviour and wouldn't speak to me for some days afterwards.

When we got to Cardiff we spent at least an hour going round and round in circles, looking for Ninian Park. I wouldn't care, we'd been there three times before, which doesn't say much for our sense of direction! Eventually we decided to dump the car in the town centre and flag down a taxi. The journey to the ground took only five minutes – we could have kicked ourselves when we saw how close it was! There was still some time left before kick-off so we went for a drink in the Ninian Park pub near the ground, and although it was heaving with Cardiff City fans there was no bother at all. In the 70th minute Neil Matthews played a suicidal back pass to the Cardiff keeper and it ended up in the back of the net. We therefore won 1-0 that day courtesy of an own-goal.

After the game, Ian and I stayed with Lynne's parents in Brecon. The town is a big army base and at that time Lynne's father was a warrant officer in the army. Lynne is a very good pool player and that evening she was challenged to a game by a lad in a pub. Coolly, she seven-balled him! He, however, was adamant that it had been a fluke. So Lynne played him again and seven-balled him for the second time!

In May 1991 we played Rochdale at Feethams in our last match of the season. After nine minutes John Borthwick flicked on a prodigious goalkick from Mark Prudhoe, David Cork chested it down and slid the ball home past Keith Welch to send the 9,160 crowd into raptures. A sweetly-struck second half penalty kick from Frank Gray sealed a 2-0 victory. As full time approached the referee saw the encroaching fans behind him and sensibly blew his whistle.

I went to Darlington Cricket Club where the players and the fans were celebrating promotion. I can recall that each of the players had to stand on a chair in the middle of the room and do a turn for the fans. When David Cork took the floor he put his finger to his lips, told everybody to be quiet, and then sang, 'We are the champions!' Unlike the game against Swansea in April 1976, which I mentioned in Chapter Two, this time we really were the champions.

Later, Ian, Trevor, Phil, Neil Parkinson and myself caught a train from Bank Top station to Bishop Auckland where Graham was holding a celebratory party. Graham had a full-size snooker table in his house and Ian tried to teach me how to play the game, with predictably disastrous results. We stayed there overnight, drinking beer and eating pizzas, and came back on Sunday with massive hangovers!

Sadly, Brian Little left the club for Leicester City after that match. His assistant Frank Gray, whose laid-back style of management was partly to blame for the club's next period of decline, replaced him.

During the summer of 1991 I went on holiday to Corfu with Ian and four other lads from Colburn. We had a great time and got wrecked every night. Our friendship, though, was certainly put to the test. When I had the skitters a few times because the food didn't agree with me I needed help and Ian didn't let me down.

At home I have a device called a 'Closimat' – you press a button and it squirts a jet of water, which cleans your backside. But when I went to Greece, with its rather primitive sanitary facilities, I needed help in that particular department. Ian never flinched, though I did hear him muttering something about Cadbury's Caramel after the ordeal was over!

On that holiday I actually went paragliding for the first time. It was like being on *Match of the Day* because I don't think any of the Greeks had seen anything like that before. They couldn't believe it when I wanted to do it and eventually there was a big audience for my maiden flight, which was quite embarrassing.

The people we stayed with were disgusted by our noisy and laddish behaviour. The first day, Ian gave me a hand to get on the toilet and, in trying to steady myself, I pulled the handrail off. That didn't go down too well with the hotel management.

On another occasion, we stacked some plastic garden chairs outside a couple's chalet door so that when they opened it all the chairs fell on top of them. I also remember the time I annoyed Ian so much that he left me sitting naked outside the chalet on the veranda. After a few such incidents, the big Greek proprietor told us he was fed up with us and fired a shotgun in the air to emphasise his point! I don't know, some people have no sense of humour.

I can honestly say that the only argument we had on that holiday was on the last night. We had a beer fight and I got a good soaking. Ian and some lads from Wigan tipped beer all over me because I'm such an easy target. I can't jump out of the way, can I? I retaliated by wetting Ian and he went into a sulk. He said I'd ruined his decent trousers. 'Well,' I said, 'Look at *my* trousers.' Eventually he saw the funny side of it.

The new football season brought the usual initial wave of optimism that was soon dashed by a string of defeats. In October 1991 I went to Exeter again with John Gray, masochist that I am, and we experienced yet more trouble when a cocky steward asked us to move from the sparsely-populated away end. I asked, 'Do you mind if I finish my drink first and then I'll gladly move.' I had a cup of hot Bovril in one hand and a pie in the other and it was ten minutes before kick-off. John remarked, 'Come on mate, be reasonable, there are only twenty people in the away end.' The steward, however, was unmoved and said, 'Any more lip from you and you'll be chucked out,' and he made me move straight away, which meant that I had to sit amongst the home fans.

As a disabled football fan, this certainly wasn't the first example of discrimination and shabby treatment that I'd encountered on my travels. You will recall my argument with the steward at West Ham, who turned me away from Upton Park on safety grounds. The Exeter steward seemed to have been cast from the same mould – he was acting like a little Hitler who wouldn't listen to reason. He was getting a cheap thrill by giving John and me unnecessary hassle. No wonder some of my mates didn't like pushing my wheelchair to football matches – you could hardly blame them.

The steward's attitude seemed all the more stupid to me since the away end was virtually empty. You could have understood his point of view if that section of the ground had been full. It seemed to me that his whole attitude was a case of bureaucracy gone mad. Sometimes common sense should prevail. Because of the steward's inflexible nature I ended up being put in the disabled area amongst the home fans where some idiots who were standing behind me thought it would be fun to spit at me.

As I've already said, I fully accept that if the away end happens to be full and it isn't possible to accommodate my wheelchair I'll gladly go in the disabled section. But to be asked to move when there's no need is totally unacceptable. Why should I have to go in the bloody awful home end where people spit at you, are bad mannered and where I can't be with my friends? If I'd been a woman or a member of any of the ethnic minorities I wouldn't have been asked to move to another part of the ground, now would I?

To add insult to injury I was overcharged by two pounds – the home fans paid £5 whereas I was charged £7 admittance. That was against the Football League rules. Afterwards, I wrote a letter of complaint to the Exeter manager, Alan Ball, but Exeter saw nothing wrong with my treatment. I then wrote to the Football League at Lytham St Anne's and they upheld my complaint.

I certainly don't like Exeter City, the club or their ramshackle ground. In my opinion, they should knock the place down as soon as possible and I sincerely hope they are relegated. I must apologise for this lengthy tirade, but I have to say that they are the worst club I've ever visited in my life. Football has to change and Exeter City are about fifty years behind the times.

To complete a miserable day, we lost 4-1, Steve Moran scoring all four of the Grecians' goals on twelve, fourteen, sixty and eighty minutes with Lee Ellison grabbing our consolation goal from the penalty spot after thirty-six minutes. Not only that, Jim Willis was sent off for the Quakers after seventy-seven minutes for persistently fouling Moran. This was the measure of our season and by May we finished bottom of the Third Division, by which time Ray Hankin had replaced the ineffectual Frank Gray.

The Quakers had entered yet another downward cycle with a succession of managers coming and going in the next few years, all to no avail. The club lurched from one extreme to another, and under the authoritarian regime of Billy McEwan we saw the departure of Kevan Smith on a free transfer. Even the club's business dealings were undermined by black humour – we bought a second-hand stand from Stockton racecourse with the intention of roofing over the Polam Lane end of the ground, only to find out that we couldn't afford to erect it! But these irritations were as nothing, compared to what fate had in store for me. It was time for football to take a back seat.

Chapter 11

When I got my job with Farmway Ltd in Darlington, I was fortunate that my friend and colleague, Stephen Luck, was able to give me a lift home every day. My mother usually left the front door off the latch, but one day in February 1992 I returned to find my front door locked. I knew immediately that something was wrong. It was a weird and sickening feeling.

After Stephen had knocked repeatedly on the door without any reply I said, 'Go round the back and see where my mother is.' I tried to convince myself that she might have just popped out to the shops for something, but I didn't really believe that for one moment. When Stephen came back his face was deathly white and he said, 'Paul, your mam's lying on the floor.' In sheer panic he ran round to the back of the house again; to be truthful, neither of us knew what to do.

At that moment one of our neighbours happened to be walking past, and I told him what was wrong. While I was speaking to him I noticed that my bedroom window had been left open and my neighbour offered to climb in.

You can imagine the scene. There I was sitting outside the front door wondering whether or not my mother was still alive. When my neighbour did eventually climb in through the window to check on her condition it seemed like an eternity before he opened the front door and I saw her lying on the floor, with blood everywhere. At first I thought she'd been mugged. My whole world seemed to fall apart. Although I didn't know it at the time, my nice little life was about to change beyond belief.

Before the ambulance arrived to take my mother to the hospital, I telephoned Alison and my stepsisters. I don't think any of my stepsisters actually believed me when I broke the dreadful news. Stephen drove me to the hospital where a doctor eventually told me that my mother had suffered a massive stroke.

While my mother was in hospital, one of my friends, Neil Parkinson, stayed with me, and then Alison looked after me for a while. Each night after work I visited my mother in hospital. A month passed and she was discharged, but she wasn't the same person any more. Despite undergoing a period of home-based physiotherapy and drug treatment, she deteriorated quickly. Between 1992 and 1994 she was in hospital four or five times and suffered as many as twelve strokes. Eventually, in April 1992 I managed to get some home carers in to help me.

As the year progressed my mother started to display the first symptoms of Alzheimer's disease, such as general forgetfulness and irrational behaviour.

What made this situation even more unbearable was the fact that I had no information supplied to me by the medical profession or Social Services which would give me some sort of guidance on how to cope with my mother's confused behaviour. Nor was I referred to any organisations or support groups for the relatives of stroke victims or those suffering from Alzheimer's disease.

To make matters worse, my mother resented me having any outside help because she thought they were interfering and trying to take over. As a result, the situation deteriorated to such an extent that I was finding myself on my own for longer and longer periods, having to look after her virtually single-handed. Although Alison and three of my stepsisters did come round on a fairly regular basis they could go home and shut their front doors whereas I just never seemed to get a break.

That Christmas my mother and I were invited to stay at Alison's, but unfortunately my mother upset the two children with her fits of temper. Alison was rushed off her feet and vowed, never again. I think she was surprised to discover just what a handful my mother could be.

I certainly don't regret having cared for my mother, now that I've overcome many of my own problems, but thinking about it rationally, I believe that this stressful time sowed the seeds for my own subsequent nervous breakdown. I was awake most nights looking after her and then had to go to work the next morning. That was the situation for two and a half years. It was hardly a recipe for my own physical and mental health.

As I've said, I don't regret having done this because I loved my mother to bits, and if I had to make the same decision again I would still have tried to care for her, to the best of my ability. But the strain was unbearable. For instance, she would get up in the middle of the night and say, 'Paul, your dinner is ready.' I would therefore have to sit down and eat the meal she had cooked simply not to upset her.

At other times she'd wake me up and ask, 'Where's my purse?' to which I'd reply, 'Under your pillow.' Then she would ask me where her jewellery was, so I'd have to get up and show her, otherwise she'd go to look for it herself. Some nights this might happen a dozen times, so in the end I used to leave all her personal belongings in her bedroom where she could find them. When I was at work she'd ring me to ask, 'Paul, how do you switch the fire on?' or 'What time are you coming home from work?'

You can't imagine the immense mental strain that I had to endure. There I was, a disabled man with problems of my own, struggling to look after my mother as well. It was a situation that I wasn't able to handle on my own and

I felt that I wasn't getting enough support from my own family.

I felt that my stepsisters in particular let me down in a big way. Up until the onset of my mother's illness they had treated me civilly, but when I asked them for assistance they seemed to balk at the suggestion. Perhaps they resented the fact that my mother had walked out on them when they were children. Maybe that accounts for their behaviour.

Whatever the reasons might have been, I found myself working full time and coming home to my unpredictable and irrational mother. I didn't know whether she would be in a good or a bad mood from one moment to the next. She was so confused that she didn't know where she was half the time. On one occasion she even thought I was her husband.

In August 1993 she had another stroke but the doctor who came out to see her wouldn't admit her into hospital and gave her a sleeping pill instead. He didn't seem to consider the problem of a disabled person being responsible for the welfare of someone who was seriously ill and mentally confused. He told me that he'd give her a pill and that she'd be knocked out till morning, but his prognosis was wrong.

Later that night I was in bed listening to the phone-in programme on the local station, TFM Radio, when I heard a loud thud. My mother had fallen out of bed. There I was, unable to walk unaided, with a mother who needed to use a Zimmer frame to get about. When I managed to reach her I found that she had sustained a deep cut on the back of her head.

I haven't got a lot of strength in my hands so I got some toilet tissue and tried to stop the bleeding by wrapping it round her head, but I just couldn't manage it. The blood was oozing out between my fingers. It was horrific. As a last resort, I told her to keep hold of it, but she didn't understand me and kept pulling the tissue off.

In the end I took a gamble and left her for a few minutes while I telephoned one of my stepsisters. She came round within about ten minutes to find me and my mother covered in blood. This was one of those defining moments when I knew that I couldn't give my mother the care that she needed.

My stepsister took her to the hospital and we were confident that they'd keep her in, at least overnight. But they didn't. To my utter amazement they bandaged her head and sent her home, even though they were in full possession of the facts. That really made me wonder what on earth the Health Service was all about. They knew my mother had had a stroke the previous day, and that she had fallen out of bed due to a doctor's negligence and split her head open, and yet they were quite prepared to send her home.

After my mother's return she continued to deteriorate. By this time her recent memory had all but gone and her lucid moments were becoming fewer and fewer. For example, she used to have quite a lot of money in her purse, but this would regularly disappear, for no apparent reason. Naturally, I can't accuse anyone of stealing it, because my mother might have simply given it away unwittingly.

It broke my heart to see someone I loved so much withering away. I would often ring my good friend Robbo if I needed help in putting my mother to bed. I'd met him in 1990, and as a result of going to football matches together we'd became firm friends. His willingness to lend a hand was a sharp contrast to my own family.

In October 1993 I took another step towards greater independence when I exercised my right to buy the flat we rented from the council and obtained a mortgage. By December 1993 I was a physical and mental wreck, so much so that my father came round to cook the Christmas dinner. My mother was in a terrible mood and I felt very alone.

When Stephen Lowson returned from Cambridge for the Christmas holiday he couldn't believe my mother's rapid decline. I went with him to the match against Carlisle United on Boxing Day, a dull game that was littered with defensive errors. Our inconsistent form under the new manager, Alan Murray, continued to plague us and we suffered a dispiriting 3-1 defeat, with Paul Cross replying for the Quakers.[1] During that week Stephen and I had a few nights out. I also went to Ian's house on New Year's Eve, but with my mother being in such a state I wasn't able to stay.

I pleaded for more help for my mother, but she steadfastly refused any assistance that was offered, so I had to care for her as best I could. Social Services suggested respite care as a possible solution, and we tried it over a weekend. My mother, however, didn't like it and so I decided not to repeat the experiment.

What concerned me most was that my mother was being left on her own during the day while I was at work. Although someone would come to see her at about half past nine to get her dressed and make her breakfast, between ten in the morning and five in the afternoon she was left to her own devices. When I learned that my request for more day care had been turned down, I naturally felt pretty depressed.

One night, in February 1994, I went for a drink with John Gray. Since he lives just round the corner from me and is still a single lad I probably see

[1]By May 1994 we finished second from bottom of the division.

more of him than any of my other mates. I know that if I'm bored I can ring him and he'll come round for a chat or go out with me to the pub.

That night, while we were out, John kept asking me if I was all right. He said later that he could tell something was wrong. I managed to stay sober that night and I remember him offering to sit and talk, but I said that I was fine.

After he left I took 25 co-proxamols, which are a type of painkiller, and promptly fell asleep. Three hours later, I woke up feeling really odd and then remembered what I'd done. I struggled to the telephone and rang for an ambulance; it seemed to be there within minutes.

When I got to the hospital, though, I refused all treatment. In desperation, the doctor on duty rang Alison and told her to come as quickly as possible. When she arrived we both burst into tears. She said that she hadn't realised how bad things had become.

Eventually, after much persuasion, she got me to accept the treatment. I was given some medicine that made me vomit all night. I remember that a nurse came and talked to me; she lay down beside me on the bed and I poured out the whole story of how I'd looked after my mother for two years and about her worsening condition. We talked for what seemed like hours. Her final comment was, 'Nothing is worth dying for, Paul.'

On reflection, I don't consider this to have been a genuine suicide attempt. It was simply a cry for help, a way of drawing attention to my plight.

I was released from hospital the following day and John came round to see me straight away. He was very upset.

After that harrowing period I did eventually get proper night care for my mother and a woman called Jane entered my life. She became my girlfriend – more of her later.

It was during this period of my life that I also began to experience occasional spasms in my limbs, and this is still the case today. Although medication was available to me at the time, in practice I didn't bother taking it because of the irritating side-effects, and I've managed to do without it to this day. The medical profession were, however, quite unimpressed by my decision to ignore their well-meant advice. My doctor even warned me that the frequency and intensity of these spasms would get worse over time, but my preferred option was to be alert and able to work rather than constantly drowsy and lethargic.

Due to this problem it was quite natural that I would sometimes become angry and frustrated when I was making a cup of tea and dropped it as a result of a spasm. But, having cursed my fill, I usually ended up laughing at myself and making another. Even so, the sheer inconvenience of not being able to do the sort of practical tasks that most people take for granted was very infuriating. That's why I needed home care during this period not only for my mother but also for myself.

By this time, I had a home carer called Trish who is a very nice lady. We're still good friends today. She certainly used to put up with a lot from my mother. I can remember that at tea time my mother always moaned about her food. It was either too hot or too cold. One particular night I'd just got in from work, and Trish had cooked a lovely meal with meat and vegetables: a really nice tea. Anyway, while I was tucking into mine my mother said, 'Trish, mine's too cold.' Helpful as ever, Trish said, 'No problem, Alice, I'll warm it up for you in the microwave.' Trish accordingly heated it up, but when she set the plate down on the table my mother threw it all over the floor and said, 'It's too fucking hot now.' I didn't know whether to laugh or cry and poor Trish had to clear up all the mess. Five minutes later my mother couldn't remember the incident.

Trish and I often discussed the decline in my mother's health, and the crunch came one morning when Trish found some burnt paper in my mother's bed. This convinced me to do something that ultimately made me lose my family, but I couldn't see any other choice. God knows I tried my best. After that discovery of the burnt paper I knew I would have to tell my mother that I was sorry, but I couldn't look after her any longer.

I knew I had to act decisively. I took advice from Trish, from colleagues at work, from friends and from my social worker. It was the hardest decision of my life. At the end of the day I couldn't let my mother live with me any longer. I was fraught with guilt knowing how much she wanted to stay with me. I still wanted to believe there could be a compromise.

Using Social Services as an intermediary, I arranged a meeting with the rest of my family, during which we would hopefully reach some sort of solution to my mother's long term needs. This meeting was scheduled to take place after a holiday in Ibiza. I needed a break. I was cracking up. My mother was in hospital again, so I went away for a week in August 1994.

On my return I attended the meeting at which my family and my social worker were present. I also took Dave, a colleague from work, as a witness. When it came to my turn to speak I said that if one of them would be prepared to look after my mother at the weekend I would gladly keep her at home. Since there were four of them they could have rotated this duty between them once a month. That would have been the end of the problem as far as I was concerned. I would have taken care of her for five days and used the weekend to recharge my batteries. I needed time to myself because I felt my head would explode with all the pressure.

Naturally, Alison had already offered to look after our mother at the weekend, but her living conditions were inappropriate, since she had only just moved house, and things were still in quite a state. There simply wasn't any way that Social Services would have allowed my mother to live in the same environment as a boisterous four-year-old. In any case, the bedrooms were upstairs and it would have meant my mother sleeping in the living room.

To my utter amazement, none of my stepsisters would agree to my proposal. Their excuses, in my opinion, were lame and unbelievable. One of them said her toilet was upstairs. My social worker suggested, 'We could always get you a commode.' But the idea was flatly rejected.

My pleas for help were in vain. They each said they had commitments. I replied, 'What about *my* commitments, what about *my* life?' It seemed that my happiness counted for nothing. Their behaviour reminded me of a comment that Ian had once made: 'You can choose your friends but you can't choose your family.'

Maybe I should have been stronger and put my foot down earlier, but the truth is I didn't because I loved my mother so much. But, when I learned that none of my stepsisters would have her even for a weekend, I dug in my heels and refused to look after her any longer. This was at the end of October 1994.

My stepsisters accused me of attempting to evict my mother so that I could install my girlfriend in her place. That was a gross distortion of the truth. If I'd been driven by purely selfish motives, why had I cared for my mother for more than two and a half years? I thought that my refusal to look after her would mean that Social Services would have no alternative but to admit her to a nursing home or somewhere more suitable, where she could receive the care and attention that I was unable to give her. As it turned out, she went to stay with my father instead.

When she returned to my father's house I spoke to her on the phone on a Friday night when I knew that he'd be out. I gathered from what she said that she wasn't very happy there, but I had no other choice. I just couldn't cope with looking after her.

On the 30th of November 1994, after yet another stroke, my mother died. I got a phone call from the hospital saying that I should come straight away. If I'd known before that she had only four or five weeks to live, I'd never have let her go to stay with my father. I was absolutely racked with guilt. I'll never forget the day that my mother died. I went to the hospital with Trish. When we arrived we met one of my stepsisters who informed me that my mother was dead and then just walked off. Trish was disgusted.

Stephen came up from Cambridge and stayed with me for over a week. All my mates were really supportive. It was a bad time because I knew now that Alison was all I had left of my family. Now that I'm okay and can think logically I'm glad that I lost the rest of my family and don't want to have anything to do with them ever again.

One of my stepsisters had the gall to criticise me, saying that it was my fault that my mother had died. She even called me a murderer in the hospital.

My relatives made the arrangements for the funeral, which meant that I wasn't involved in any meaningful way. They inserted an obituary notice in *The Northern Echo*. It read as follows:

HODGSON November 30 (in hospital) of Dundee Street, Darlington, Alice, aged 64 years, wife of Norman, a dear mother, mother-in-law, nana and great nana. Funeral Monday, December 5. Will friends please meet for service and cremation 3.15 p.m. at Darlington Crematorium.

I suppose it was noticeable that neither Alison nor I were mentioned by name and interesting that my father was.

On the day of the funeral my relatives told me that I couldn't accompany them in the family car. Consequently, I had to make my own way there. Luckily, all of my friends knew the score and rallied round me. I don't know where I would have been without their support. During the service at the Crematorium I sat in the middle of the chapel surrounded by my friends, including Stephen Luck, Linda and Ruth, my colleagues from Farmway. I certainly didn't want to sit next to my so-called relations. I thought the way they treated me at the funeral was an utter disgrace.

The service itself was a farce. I was horrified when the vicar referred to my father throughout as the grieving husband. Didn't he know that my mother had left him more than five years previously? Not only that, he said what a close family we were and what good daughters my stepsisters were! I was appalled – a fake picture was being created of a family, united in grief. If it hadn't been a funeral, a solemn occasion, I'd have piped up and told them all what I thought, but as it was, I kept quiet.

After the service Alison came over to me and took me to see the wreaths. That was a nice touch. I can remember feeling as though it was all a dream.

A bad dream.

After the funeral my stepsisters totally ignored me. I think now that it was a direct result of their guilt. They knew that I'd done more than any of them to care for my mother.

I was bluntly told to stay away from the reception. As a result of their behaviour, half of the funeral party came to my place instead, including my uncle Alan and aunt Janet, who offered me great moral support when I most needed it. They both stood by me because they knew that I'd done my best.

There were about twenty of us at my place. I laid on a simple buffet. I was physically exhausted and felt empty inside. Jane, my girlfriend, came round twice that day, but she didn't come to the funeral for reasons I shall explain later. That was unfortunate because I needed her that day more than ever before. After the mourners left, I went out with Neil Parkinson and got roaring drunk.

Not surprisingly, I had the worst Christmas ever at Alison's. I had to make an effort for the sake of her kids though, because they naturally didn't understand what had happened. Since my mother's death I haven't spoken to those members of my family with whom I fell out. I only keep in touch with my father and my sister now. As for the others, I've nothing further to say.

Chapter 12

The reader may have been surprised to learn from the previous chapter, that the first time I personally received home care during the day was the year that my mother became ill. Until that time it was my mother who paid the bills, did the shopping, cooked my meals, washed my clothes and helped me in the morning to get ready for work.

When she was no longer able to do these things it became apparent that, in order to be able to cope successfully with the restrictions imposed upon me by my physical disability, and to be able to live as normal a life as possible, I required daily assistance from Social Services with these basic household chores. Since I lack coordination in my hands I also needed help in the morning with shaving, washing my hair and such minor details as fastening my shoelaces and the buttons on my shirt before my taxi arrived to take me to work.

Although I liked my first local authority home carer, I soon formed the impression that the administration of the home care service was ad hoc, and that many of the staff in the Social Services department were set in their ways. As a young, working man I considered them to be inflexible and bureaucratic. Many of them found it difficult to believe that I was capable of holding down a full time job. Some of them were patronising towards me and I didn't like that at all. In short, they didn't have any disability etiquette.

The attitude of some home carers reminded me of those ignorant and superficial people who casually glance at the cover of a book and then put it to one side instead of reading the contents. If there's one thing I can't stand it's people who talk down to me; I'm probably more intelligent than they are, anyway.

I don't think these home carers understood my lifestyle sufficiently as they were more used to looking after retired people. I can imagine that for many of the older carers it was probably a big culture shock working with a young man. Coming face to face with me, someone who swore frequently, was sexually active, got drunk and suffered from hangovers must have been quite disconcerting. You could almost hear them saying to themselves: 'Disabled people shouldn't go out drinking; disabled people shouldn't use obscene language; disabled people shouldn't have sex.' But why not? Maybe they thought I should have entered a monastery and become a monk.

Not that their uncomprehending attitude was in any way out of the ordinary, in my experience. I can remember one amusing incident that occurred in Catterick one New Year's Eve when I stayed at Ian's.

I'd met a woman in a nightclub, chatted to her for hours and then invited her back to Ian's house for a party. Afterwards, we slept together on the floor. Later, she said to me, 'I didn't realise that you'd be able to have sex.' So I asked her, 'Why?' She replied that her mother and father had told her that people in wheelchairs couldn't have sex. I laughed and said, 'Now you can go home and tell them the truth.' I often wonder now if she only went with me to prove something to herself. I did see her a few times afterwards, though, and I shall have more to say on the subject of sexuality in the following chapter.

Many home care assistants from the Social Services department seemed to have the same kind of blinkered attitude as that girl in the Catterick nightclub. Overall, my experiences of private provision were more favourable, with a few notable exceptions.

For example, one young girl who was sent to me from the private nursing home that provided my mother's night care actually woke *me* up when my mother had a fit. I got the distinct impression that some of these private companies and even the local authority were sometimes sending people who appeared to be woefully inexperienced. I recall another young girl from the same organisation who, when asked what she would do if my mother took ill, said she'd wake me up to deal with the problem, despite the fact that *she* was being paid to look after her. I was very surprised by this answer!

Just before my mother died in 1994 I decided to go private for my own day care as well because I was fed up with different people coming into my house with their old-fashioned and narrow-minded attitudes. Besides, the work wasn't being done properly and there was no continuity. I had Trish coming each morning of the week, four others in the afternoon and another person at the weekend, so altogether I had six carers. That was no damned good to me; not only was it a highly stressful experience, I soon discovered that half of them didn't really want to come to me in the first place.

In November 1994 I was nursing a broken hand after I'd been accidentally tipped out of my wheelchair at Hartlepool. Robbo and I were late for the game, and when he stumbled in a pothole I flew out of my chair and he fell on top of me. My face was quite badly cut and my hand was hurting like hell. The more the game went on the more my hand throbbed, but like a true professional I was determined to watch the match and play through the pain barrier! It was worth it, too, because we won 2-0, with a brace of goals from Gavin Worboys on fifty-eight and eighty-eight minutes.

The day after, though, I went to the hospital with Jane to have my hand x-rayed and they confirmed that it was broken. Naturally, I couldn't get into bed unaided, so I asked one of my carers to come round. She turned up so drunk I don't know how she managed to drive to my house. She staggered in with a can of beer in her hand and yet *she* was supposed to be putting *me* to bed.

In hindsight, I think she had some personal problems. One night she offered me sex, but I turned it down because she was a young girl, and I didn't want to become involved with someone else while I was seeing Jane. Unfortunately, I was pretty certain that she took some money out of my drawer. She got the sack eventually, and yet I trusted her.

When a good friend died, she went with me to the funeral. You could say that we were fairly close, though not in a sexual sense. She came round for dinner sometimes when she was off duty. So I felt badly let down and betrayed when she took the money. If only she'd asked me I'd have gladly given her a loan.

However, this case was the exception rather than the rule, and in the main I liked the staff from that particular private nursing home. I got very close to another carer from the same company and I know this made Jane jealous. We went out for meals together and to the pictures once or twice. I suppose that was against the rules, but we didn't do anything illegal as it was in our own time, so I couldn't see anything wrong with it. Yet such behaviour tended to be frowned upon.

I recall one young girl from another agency who was absolutely useless. She was probably the worst carer I've ever had. One day we went shopping to the local supermarket and she assured me that she had the house key in her pocket. We spent a small fortune on groceries and when we returned home she couldn't find the key. I was locked out of my own house and I had to ask her to go to Jane's place to get my spare key.

I also remember coming home one night absolutely starving and ready for my tea. I thought it was taking rather a long time for the meal to appear, so I went into the kitchen to find her staring at the microwave with a puzzled expression on her face. When I asked, 'What's wrong?' she replied, 'The microwave doesn't work.' I took one look at it and said, 'It might help if you switched it on!'

On another occasion, the same girl left all the rubbish bagged up in the middle of the kitchen floor after she'd emptied the bins. I bumped into it, nearly tipping myself out of my wheelchair. I could quite easily have broken my neck through her carelessness. She just had no commonsense at all. One day she went home and left all my windows open so I had to phone Robbo to come and shut them for me. She couldn't cook, never cleaned up properly, and the carer who came the following morning had to put right her mistakes from the previous day. I really don't know how the hell she got the job in the first place.

While another girl was working for me, money went missing, but, like a fool, I turned a blind eye. Given my low wage at the time, I needed to have a lodger just to keep my head above water and meet the mortgage repayments on the flat. Of course this meant that I was particularly vulnerable if my lodgers happened to be dishonest.

The carer cleverly managed to shift the blame for the missing money on to my lodger. This continued for quite a while, and money was also disappearing regularly from my bank account as well. There I was spending less and less and yet my overdraft was increasing.

The trouble is that most of the banks in Darlington are well nigh inaccessible to someone in a wheelchair. When I needed to draw money out I found that the cash-machines were invariably too high and awkward for me to reach, so I gave the girl my PIN number so that she could go to the bank for me. This was a mistake. I vowed that I would never do that again.

Everything came to a head when I received a phone bill for £158. I gave the girl £100 in phone stamps and the rest in cash. In the days that followed I repeatedly asked her for the bill. Eventually I was suspicious and I got Jane to ring BT to see if my bill had been paid in full. To my horror I discovered that although the £100 in phone stamps had been paid the £58 was still outstanding. Although at first the girl denied it, she eventually admitted that she hadn't paid the £58. Fortunately, the police recovered the money for me. The sad thing was that if she had needed the money so badly I would have given her a loan. She, too, was sacked for breach of contract.

Imagine if I'd been an elderly person who didn't have their wits about them or someone with severe learning difficulties who didn't understand the value of money. I could have been robbed blind and I wouldn't even have known. That scared me. It's sad when someone takes advantage like that. Even though I was partly to blame for what happened, that experience taught me a lesson I'll never forget. Because carers are put in such a unique position of trust, I would certainly advocate a more rigorous screening process before they are employed.

What I did from then on was to make sure that any money I gave my carer and every cheque I wrote was logged and fully accounted for. Don't get me wrong, I'm not saying that I didn't trust them, it's just that I was making sure that I'd never leave myself open to be abused like that again.

Over the years things have improved to a certain extent, and the Social

Services provision has had to adapt to the changes in people's circumstances; they now have to be more flexible in their approach. About ten years ago a home help would start work at nine and finish at twelve. But now there are more and more people with different needs. As a result, the whole situation has changed for the better, and as an acknowledgement of their greater responsibility home helps are now known as home carers.

Despite these welcome changes, I still feel that the basic *organisation* of home care services is fundamentally flawed in one important respect. From what I've said, you'll have gathered that the *needs* of younger disabled people are radically different from those of, say, older retired people. That's why I believe that there should be two distinct departments – one catering solely for younger physically disabled people and another for the elderly, whether they happen to be disabled or not.

In my opinion, Community Care is a good thing, especially if it means getting disabled people or the mentally ill out of residential homes and institutions, which belong to a more intolerant era. When problems occur with resettling people back into the community the underlying cause is usually the lack of resources – it is clearly a foolish and dangerous practice to view Community Care merely as the cheapest option. If my experiences are anything to go by, another factor that seems to have been inadequately addressed in the early years was the statutory regulation and inspection of care providers.

Community Care isn't the answer for everyone. In certain circumstances a form of residential care or even secure accommodation is the only realistic option. I'm thinking here of those few individuals who are either profoundly disabled or suffering from severe psychiatric disorders which make them a danger to themselves or the general public. I also think it's unfair to expect people with mild learning difficulties, who have been institutionalised over the years, to suddenly live in the community with only a minimum of supervision. They clearly need a lot of support, both in terms of financial and personal assistance, before they can achieve a degree of independence.

I've been lucky in that my mother taught me to be independent, and I'm eternally grateful to her for that. There was never any question of my going into an institution. I know some disabled people whose mobility allowance is spent on a car for their parents. In other words, some parents are reliant on their son or daughter's money when it's not even legally theirs in the first place.

I also know some disabled adults who only get a few pounds a week pocket money, and that's surely no way to be treated. The parents become so dependent on the money that they can't afford to give it back. I know another disabled person who is eager to leave home and live on her own, but her mother can't afford to let her go, so she gets a lot of emotional blackmail. Why the hell should she have to live at home with her mother all her life?

Another disabled friend once told me of a person she knew in her thirties. Her father used to change her nappy in the living room in front of everybody. He once told her that if she ever had sex with a man it would kill her. I'm lucky in that I had one decent parent but quite a lot of parents mollycoddle their disabled children and do everything for them. But what happens when the parents die? The son or daughter ends up in an institution.

Attitudes to disability amongst able-bodied people also have to change. Where women are concerned, the sight of my wheelchair puts many of them off. Even if they pluck up the courage to speak to me, they tend to feel sorry for me or want to mother me, which is the last thing I need. There have been times, for example, when I've spoken to a woman in a nightclub and I've seen her shudder in disgust and almost say, 'Ugh,' because I had the audacity to chat her up. But why such a negative reaction in the first place?

Regrettably, there must be quite a lot of disabled people who, through no fault of their own, might never have sex during their lives, and that's a shame. I hope this book makes it abundantly clear that people like me who happen to be in a wheelchair are sexual beings and have needs like everyone else. I think the following chapter will demonstrate this.

Chapter 13

The time has now come for me to tell you more about the unusual circumstances in which I met my former girlfriend, Jane, and why I have attempted to conceal her identity from the reader. I hope she realises that this account of our relationship has not been written as a personal vendetta, but only to tell the truth about what happened between us.

You will recall that in April 1994 I obtained more help in the form of night care for my mother, and some time after that Jane came to nurse her. I must admit that I was attracted to Jane instantly. Later, when I found out that she was married, my desire grew even stronger. About three weeks after I met her I was getting over an attack of shingles and she offered to give me a massage. I thought, 'Why not?' and one thing led to another. We didn't do much that particular night, apart from kissing and cuddling, but were both greatly tempted.

The more Jane came round to look after my mother, the closer we grew, and within a month we were sleeping together. We used to meet at lunchtime, in a pub on the outskirts of Darlington, and by June we were seeing each other almost every day.

As our relationship developed I discovered that Jane had problems of her own and was bored and dissatisfied with her marriage. She admitted to me that she'd already had an affair long before I met her. She'd married in her late teens, and explained to me that, whereas she still liked to go out in the evening and socialise, her husband was content to stay at home watching television. Clearly, she seemed to be craving some illicit excitement, and it wasn't long before the dangers of our secret liaison became all too apparent to both of us.

The first time we made love, I readily admit, was a complete disaster – I was far too nervous, but the second time was a much more satisfying experience for both of us. Our preferred means of birth control in those early days was the withdrawal method, since I can't use a condom because it's just too painful. Later we decided that this form of contraception was simply too risky so Jane was fitted with a coil.

Jane was a very good lover and was certainly not afraid to experiment. For example, we once had sex in the wheelchair, which was a massive turn-on for me. Even if I live to be ninety I don't think any woman will excite me as much as she did. She would try anything. In fact, Jane once said that I was the best lover she had ever had, though I suppose that is the kind of thing a woman is likely to say to the man who happens to be in bed with her at the time. There was a definite sexual rapport between us.

In August, as a result of a chance remark my mother let slip, my stepsisters made it clear that they were suspicious of our relationship and it was therefore only a matter of time before we were both summoned to a meeting with Jane's employer to explain our behaviour.

I must say, I found this formal enquiry a total farce. I went with Dave, my colleague from work. He was someone I could trust and he acted as a witness. Jane and I were interviewed separately, almost as if we were criminals, which I found quite strange. We were two consenting adults, after all.

I was asked to explain my sex life with Jane. I admitted that we were having an affair – I could hardly deny it – but in order to protect my mother, I vehemently denied that we were sleeping together at my house. I had to lie on that occasion for the sake of my mother's health, because the upset caused by these accusations could well have aggravated her condition. It appeared that some of Jane's colleagues overheard my conversation with the centre manager. That was an awful state of affairs. There was simply no confidentiality at all, and I now know it was a big mistake to have attended the enquiry in the first place. I should never have done that. But at the time I felt it was the right thing to do.

It was pretty bad, I can't deny it, and I was accused of all sorts of things. Although we did sleep together when Jane was on duty, my mother was never in any danger. She was asleep most of the time and even if she did happen to wake up and call for help Jane would put her clothes back on and see to her needs. My mother was consequently none the wiser. Jane and I were two people who were attracted to each other. I was only human, after all. I don't condone what I did, it was clearly wrong, but these things happen in life.

As a result of the enquiry, it seemed that nearly everybody in the immediate area got to hear about our relationship and Jane was the talk of her neighbourhood for several months. The gossip didn't particularly bother me, but it obviously affected Jane.

She was asked to leave her post, which she did, and her husband discovered that she had resigned because of our affair. In September she actually told him about us. According to her, he was devastated and couldn't handle the thought of someone in a wheelchair taking away his wife.

She also claimed that her husband had never been able to satisfy her sexually, words that were to haunt me later. Really, looking back on it now, I should have known then that if she could speak so scornfully of her husband behind his back what might she say about me to other men in the future? But you don't really consider those things too deeply at the time.

Jane eventually left her husband for a while. Shortly afterwards he booked a second honeymoon so that they could get back together. But Jane was living a big lie. She'd even promised her husband, swearing on her children's lives, never to see me again. In reality, though, we never stopped seeing each other. She only stayed with him because they had a nice house and a nice car and he was earning a good wage. She even admitted as much in a conversation with two of my home care assistants – when she was asked why she wouldn't leave her husband for me she implied that it was because I wouldn't be able to offer her the same standard of living. I thought that was a terrible admission to make, but at the time I didn't want to think about its possible implications for our relationship.

During this period my sister was in the process of moving house. The night before Jane and her husband were due to go on the second honeymoon Jane came to see me. We went round to Alison's empty house and must have had sex in nearly every one of the downstairs rooms. I now find it quite hard to believe that someone about to go on a second honeymoon with her husband could do that.

Jane told me later that the second honeymoon was a nightmare. All she could do was think about me; and during that period her husband became more and more possessive. I missed her deeply that week, more than I had ever missed anyone before.

I think half of the carers who came to my house afterwards knew what had gone on between Jane and me, so they were wary of turning up on my doorstep. But what exactly were they afraid of? Just because I had slept with one carer didn't mean I would sleep with them all. Life isn't like that.

Eventually the gossip died down and people thought that we'd stopped seeing each other. Even Jane's mother didn't know we were still meeting until Jane came out with the truth. Eventually the whole of Jane's family knew what was going on, with the exception of her husband. He must have been either very stupid or very naive. I think it was probably the latter.

We continued to see each other regularly, and when Jane's husband started working night shifts our meetings were easier to arrange. Having asked her mother to babysit, Jane would come round to my house. In one way Jane's mother was quite supportive, knowing that her daughter was coming to see me, but on the other hand she made it quite clear from the outset that she disapproved of the relationship.

In fact, almost all of her family were opposed to it. For example, an aunt of Jane's told her that if she left her husband for me she might lose her children because of my disability. That would never have been the case, but I think this is where Jane's problem with my disability originated. Sadly, some of Jane's family were bigoted towards me, and that was a shame.

By 1995 I was desperately ill, an alcoholic in all but name. I was drinking half a bottle of vodka and six cans of lager most nights after work, a state of affairs that was to drag on for nearly a year and a half.

To celebrate my thirtieth birthday, my good friend John Gray helped to arrange a big party, and altogether nearly a hundred people turned up, an attendance that certainly surprised me. You will recall that only three months previously my mother had died, so I was still feeling pretty depressed at the time and in need of a lift.

However, five of my closest friends each told me a very similar story about Jane the next day. She'd apparently been chatting up different men, though I wasn't aware of it at the time because I was so drunk. When I confronted her, she denied it and said that I was being silly. Like a fool I believed her. Looking back now, why would five good friends whom I'd known for years make false accusations about her behaviour? The incident was however conveniently swept under the carpet.

Three days after my birthday party I took an overdose. I'd simply had enough of life. I couldn't handle the guilt any more. The mental strain of caring for my mother and my recent bereavement completely overwhelmed me. Having been called a murderer also stuck in my mind.

Fortunately, I rang someone up after I'd taken the overdose, for some reason that I can't remember now. My weekend carer gave me the kiss of life, after which I was rushed to hospital.

I took 170 tablets of a muscle relaxant drug called Baclofen. I was in intensive care and stopped breathing several times. They pumped out my stomach and I was put on a ventilator. I couldn't breathe properly for ages. The results of the toxicology tests were sent to the National Poisons' Department in Edinburgh. I have the dubious distinction of being the only person to have survived after having taken more than a hundred of these tablets, but that is not a record to be proud of.

One quality I particularly admire in my friends is their unswerving loyalty, and during this period John, Steve Tupling, Ian and his wife Lynne were all great to me. John loyally visited me every night I was in hospital. Jane, too, stuck by me, risking everything to see me. I'll never forget her for that.

While I was in hospital I was so delirious that I didn't even recognise John at first when he came to see me. He said that I asked him to draw crosses on his hand with a pen, which he later washed off. I was admitted to Winterton psychiatric hospital for two days to be assessed without the benefit of medication. My friend, Pat Foggin, who works for *Scope*, came to see me there. When Pat asked one of the doctors if I'd recover he said that he wasn't sure. No one had taken so many Baclofen tablets before and lived. They just couldn't tell what sort of lasting damage the drug might have on my body. Altogether, I was in hospital for about a month and my friends all came to see me regularly. Ian visited me nearly every day. When I was discharged, I rang the Samaritans quite often and had supportive conversations with a girl called Lizzie for hours at a stretch.

I left hospital on a Friday and, unlikely as it may seem, I sat the first exam of my GNVQ Advanced Business Studies course the following Monday. Farmway had suggested that I could enrol early that year at Darlington College of Technology, so I took advantage of their offer.

Naturally, having missed twelve weeks of lectures altogether, nobody expected me to turn up. No one knew what had been wrong with me, apart from my tutor. I kept a lot of my problems to myself. But I did turn up for the exams, and although I didn't do any revision, because I was too ill, I managed to pass five out of the six papers. I came out with a merit, which wasn't too bad, considering the harrowing events that took place during that eventful year.

I was really pleased with my achievement, retook the Finance paper at the end of term and passed it with ease. When I sat my exams, rather than using an adapted keyboard as I had in the past, I dictated the answers, and for this I was allowed extra time.

Even though I'd been discharged from hospital I was off work for another six weeks, and during this time Ian and I talked for hours on the phone, often into the early hours of the morning. When I couldn't face going to away matches on the supporters' coach he took me in his car. I still didn't feel right in myself; I should have accepted more help than I did, and this was something which I only acknowledged after I took my third, and last overdose, nearly two years later. It was some time before I could truly say that I was my old self again.

As a result of what had happened in my personal life during those eventful years since the onset of my mother's illness, my psychiatrist later told me that I'd suffered a severe nervous breakdown, so severe, that in nine out of ten cases, a full recovery would be out of the question. He was amazed that I was still holding down my job and could hardly believe that I had managed to keep all the inner turmoil to myself and not let it affect my work or my studies to any significant degree.

In an attempt to put our relationship on a more stable footing, Jane finally promised to come clean with her husband. In September she did just that, but was pushed into it by the threatening phone calls we were both receiving. We concluded that the caller was someone who used to work with Jane. This person said that, unless Jane did the decent thing by her husband, she would tell him about our affair. Jane therefore told her husband that she had been seeing me again, after having met up by chance in a local pub. This was a lie because she had never stopped seeing me. She didn't even have the guts to tell the guy the truth. He was obviously devastated by this latest revelation.

Chapter 14

Even during my stormy relationship with Jane, football still provided the one unifying factor in my life. If season 1994-95 had been a disappointment, with Alan Murray predictably sacked at the beginning of March and a final position in the league of third from bottom, season 1995-96, under the untried managerial team of Jim Platt and David Hodgson, heralded another upturn in the fortunes of Darlington FC. Jane disliked me wasting money on going to football matches, so I missed more games than usual that season. However, in September I was involved in yet another sponsored wheelchair push to Hartlepool, which I will now recount.

The words 'disability' and 'charity' very often seem to exist side by side like 'fish' and 'chips.' Ideally, state support for people who happen to be born with a disability should be sufficient to make charitable handouts unnecessary, but in practice it isn't, which means getting involved yourself and making things happen. I must admit that I'm very much against charity on a personal level – I certainly don't consider myself to be a charity case – but on this particular occasion I was actually helping someone else who was less fortunate than I was.

When Ian and I embarked on a journey from the Colburn Lodge pub in Catterick, North Yorkshire, to Hartlepool, a distance of some 40-odd miles, we were spurred on by the plight of a little girl called Sharah-Lea Minshull. She lived in Catterick and had been disabled since birth with cerebral palsy. We planned to give half the money that we raised to her appeal, since she needed some special equipment in order to help her speak. The rest of the money was to be donated to the special baby care unit at Darlington Memorial Hospital, which was where Ian's twin girls had been cared for after they were born prematurely.

Given our starting point of Catterick Garrison, Ian and I planned the second expedition to Hartlepool like a military manoeuvre and received numerous sponsorship pledges. Jane hadn't left her husband at that time, otherwise she would have driven one of the back-up cars, so I was relieved when John Gray came to my rescue and drove one of them. Ian's brother-in-law, Darren, drove the other.

The night before we were due to set off, Jane and a lad called Aubrey, who were both roped in to give me a hand, together with Ian's brother Graeme and myself, toured the pubs in Richmond town centre collecting for the appeal with a bucket.

Jane and I went round loads of pubs and ended up having a bit of an argument. I thought she was being far too aggressive in the way she was asking people for money, almost thrusting the bucket into their faces. I feel you should ask politely and if people tell you to go away or no thank you then that's fine and that should be the end of it. But it was good of her to volunteer to help me and I was hyped up by the prospect of the wheelchair push, so that might account for my irritable behaviour towards her.

We set off from Colburn at midnight, and it was absolutely bucketing with rain, much worse than the previous push in 1991. Despite the dreadful weather we made good speed. We had two wheelchairs – my usual one and a spare in case of emergency, which stayed in one of the back-up cars. Unfortunately, John's electrics kept cutting out as a result of driving at only four miles per hour for long periods of time. As it was necessary for one of the back-up cars to stay with us throughout the journey, it being a criminal offence to do a charity walk without one in attendance, we had a problem. It was obvious that neither of the two cars would make it because the rain was badly affecting their electrics. John's car in particular, a Honda Civic, was quite old anyway and it was constantly grinding to a halt.

In the end we decided that one car would stay with us for a mile or so while the other went on ahead. Then when the first car drew level with the second the roles were reversed. So with each car taking turns to stay with us that made things much easier for us.

That night Ian and I must have talked about everything imaginable. Ian was very enthusiastic about the wheelchair push and I was excited because I knew that Jane was about to leave her husband. Little did I know that a year later it would all end in total disaster. I was going on and on about how much I loved Jane, how we would get married and how she was the best thing since sliced bread. Ian, however, sounded a note of caution and warned me not to get too over-excited.

We talked about football and anything else that happened to enter our minds while he was pushing me along. And we made good time. We did encounter one problem with the wheelchair when the wheel buckled; but that was easily remedied – we simply swapped it for the spare wheelchair in Darren's car. I remember I had some waterproofs on which Ian had borrowed from the army base at which he works, but they certainly didn't live up to their name. I was absolutely soaked to the skin. I've never been so drenched in all my life. Even my underpants were wringing wet.

We stopped off at a pub in Hartlepool called the Owton Lodge where we both got changed and put on some dry clothes. By that time I could hardly move with cramp, so the lads had to practically rip the clothes from my body. Pity that there weren't any women about at the time to see me, but I don't think I'd have been able to raise a gallop anyway! I drank a couple of pints, and then we were off again on our travels.

By this time John had left us, because he had promised to meet some friends, so from then on we operated with only one back-up car. But that was fine because by then it was daylight. We arrived at Victoria Park at about eleven o'clock and went to their Supporters' Club for a few pints, purely to avoid the risk of dehydration, you understand! I was knackered by then and could hardly stay awake. Even so, after we obtained permission, we managed to collect some more money at the gate.

Though we had both completed the same wheelchair push before, we beat our previous time, and I felt proud of our achievement because it was something that nobody could take away. A few weeks later, after all the money had been collected, we organised a band night at the Colburn Lodge, and Stephen Lowson's brother-in-law, who is the lead singer of a rockabilly group called The Skip Rats, played a gig especially in our honour.

We raised £1,000 in total and gave £500 each to Sharah-Lea and Darlington Memorial Hospital. I bottled out of handing the money over in person and got Kevan Smith to do it in my place. Steve Tupling came along that night together with Jim Platt and a few of the Darlington players.

By the time of the presentation, Jane had left her husband and was living in a rented house in Darlington. Afterwards, John, Steve, Jane and I went to the Mardi Gras where I got really drunk. However, I soon sobered up when I got back home and Jane phoned to tell me that her house had been burgled. That certainly put a damper on the whole presentation night, though it couldn't diminish the sense of achievement.

Without the invaluable assistance of John, Ian's family as a whole and especially his brother-in-law Darren, we would never have accomplished the walk and raised so much money. Too many people are on the take these days. It was nice to be able to give something back for a change, and seeing on the faces of those people at the presentation the pleasure we had given them, made it all worthwhile.

And the result of the match, I hear you ask? Well, on that particular occasion our local derby was a secondary consideration. I do recall that Mark Barnard was stretchered off after a clash of heads with Tony Canham in the first half. Really, I have to admit that I was half-asleep for most of the game, but on checking my records I find that it was a 1-1 draw with Pool scoring first through Keith Houchen on seventy-two minutes and our goal coming from Anthony Carss six minutes from time.

I must admit that I don't normally fall asleep during a match, but I remember when we played Carlisle away in September 1996, a game that we lost 1-0, my friend Roger Martin pushed my wheelchair to the ground, and I'd already had a skinful by the time we got there. Anyway, after the game he asked me if I'd enjoyed it. So I brazenly said, 'Yes', to which he replied, 'Come off it, Flipper, you were fast asleep!'

Now that I've completed the Hartlepool trek on four separate occasions it doesn't present a significant challenge any more. One day in the future, though, I would like to attempt a wheelchair push to York. But that's another story.

Chapter 15

Looking back now, when Jane left her husband and moved into the house in Darlington, our relationship started to falter. Her attitude towards my disability totally changed. If, for example, I went round to her place in my wheelchair and there happened to be some mud on the tyres she would go absolutely mad. She also blurted out on one occasion that she hated pushing me about and that she hated my disability.

Her behaviour towards me became increasingly self-centred. For instance, when she left her husband she didn't have access to a car so she talked me into leasing one through the government's Motability scheme. When her divorce settlement came through and she was able to buy herself a car, she left mine on the street outside my house, since she didn't need it any more. Another time she bought me an expensive jacket, using money that she took from our joint savings, without so much as consulting me. When I saw it I didn't even like it, but rather than take it back to the shop she cut off the price tag and threw away the bill so that I would have to keep it.

Not that I was perfect by any means in my behaviour towards her. In October 1995 Jane went to stay for a week with a female friend in Blackpool. Before she left she said that she'd pick me up from Darlington Cricket Club after the match against Gillingham. 'Don't be drunk,' she added, by way of warning.

Since she was more than an hour or so late I succumbed to temptation and bought two more pints to celebrate our 1-0 victory against the Third Division leaders, courtesy of a well-crafted Gary Bannister goal. By the time she arrived I was well-oiled, but after all this was our first win at Feethams that season! When Jane saw the state I was in she understandably stormed out of the Cricket Club, whereupon I booked a taxi and followed her back to her house. When I arrived I discovered that she'd flung the Chinese takeaway that she'd bought for us in the bin. I also happened to notice that she'd specially laid the table for our meal. We then had a row and I said something objectionable about her ex-husband, for which I received a well-deserved slap across the face. I felt awful afterwards and apologised for my behaviour because it was clearly all my fault.

Although we tried to keep the relationship going, she often made an excuse for not seeing me – her favourite one being that she was tired – and so I ended up seeing her only at weekends, despite the fact that she now lived less than a mile away from me. I thought her love for me was dying and, with the benefit of hindsight, I suppose it was.

Perhaps I expected too much from her. In any event, I'm convinced that we met at the wrong time and in the wrong circumstances. It's only fair to say that my mother's illness in conjunction with my own personal problems, not least my heavy drinking, had a detrimental effect on the eventual outcome of our relationship as I was often moody and depressed during that period. If we'd met now, the whole relationship would at least have had a better chance of standing the test of time.

One thing in particular puzzled me. After Jane left her husband it was about ten weeks before I even met her children, and I thought that was a bit odd. As a matter of fact, it was in December, because we went to see a pantomime together. She hid them from me all the time, which was sad because once I did actually meet them I liked them very much.

What made this even harder to accept was that she never explained to them that I was her boyfriend. They thought I was just a friend. When I stayed at her house I had to pretend that I was sleeping downstairs on the settee and then had to creep upstairs to her bedroom when they were fast asleep.

I spent the afternoon and evening of Christmas Day with Jane and we had a nice time together, although there was definitely something lacking, and I couldn't quite understand what it was. Jane had originally promised to spend all of Christmas Day with me and then she had changed her mind and that hurt me. In an ideal world you want to spend Christmas Day with someone you love. I felt badly let down. Rather than moaning about it, though, I decided to accept second best and went round to her place after the dinner was over.

In the New Year Jane's friend came over from Blackpool to visit her. We agreed that she would take her friend out on the Friday night and I would see Jane on Saturday. At the time the weather was awful and I was relying on Jane to pick me up in the car I had leased for that very purpose. But instead of calling for me, Jane and her friend gallivanted about in my car.

Things soon deteriorated to such an extent that my thirty-first birthday celebrations in March 1996 were a complete fiasco. I went out for a meal with Jane and a few friends, but we were both thoroughly miserable. To be absolutely truthful, I formed the impression that she didn't even want to be there at all. The moment we picked her up in the taxi I knew that something wasn't quite right. But as I was with my friends I didn't want to push the matter any further.

After an Indian meal at a local curry house, we decided to go to the Mardi Gras. Unfortunately, by this time I was feeling rather ill, though not, I hasten to add, as a result of having consumed too much alcohol. It was more a case of the rich food not agreeing with my stomach. When I asked Jane to come back home with me she steadfastly refused and we had quite an argument about it. She was determined to go to the nightclub come what may. If I'd been in her shoes, I'd have returned home, whether the person I was with was ill or not. Once again that showed her selfish attitude.

I think Jane must have realised how much she'd hurt me that night because we continued to see each other in the months that followed, but we were never as close as we had been. When we first met I used to take a day off work and we would spend the whole time in bed making love. She used to bend over backwards to be with me then, but that changed. I think that since she'd left her husband, she realised she wasn't tied to any man and revelled in her new-found freedom. And that was sad, because I did love her, and tried very hard to make the relationship work. The thought even crossed my mind that she might have been simply using me to escape from an unsatisfactory marriage.

Chapter 16

The conclusion of the 1995-96 football season did nothing for the state of my frayed nerves. On the 4th of May I travelled to Scunthorpe for the last match of the season, with memories of a previous visit still fresh in my mind – the 5-1 defeat on the 6th of May 1989 that consigned us to the Vauxhall Conference. Scunthorpe never did seem to be a happy hunting ground for the Quakers. Even the manager, Mick Buxton, was the same as last time – in his second spell at the club.

Ian picked me up in his car from my home, the only other passenger that day being Ian's brother, Graeme. We left quite early at about eleven in the morning and soon found ourselves in the midst of a convoy of cars, making the same journey as ourselves. *The Northern Echo* later spoke of two thousand Darlington fans travelling to Humberside. When we arrived at about one o'clock we parked the car near the Berkeley pub and joined the fans sitting outside in the bright sunshine. After a few pints the three of us made for Glanford Park.

I managed to get in the away end where I bumped into Stephen at half-time when the score was 2-0 to the Iron with goals from Eyre on four and thirty-five minutes respectively. Appleby then converted a penalty on sixty-one minutes, which sparked off a mass brawl amongst the home fans that spilled on to the pitch. After Carss's looping header found the net on sixty-eight minutes there was yet another pitch invasion, this time from the Darlington fans. Then McFarlane scored for the Iron on eighty-seven minutes only for Barnard to equalise a minute later. The nearest we came to getting the winner that we desperately needed was when a shot smacked against the bar in the dying minutes. We were kept back inside the ground for a good ten minutes, so that the home fans could disperse. We waited anxiously for the score from Gigg Lane, because the match there had kicked off late. When we heard that Bury had won the disappointment was tangible. Automatic promotion had eluded us and we were now at the mercy of the play-offs.

My tribulations with Jane were largely forgotten when Darlington made their historic trip to Wembley at the end of May for the Third Division Play-Off Final against Plymouth Argyle. That season we set a new record on our travels away from Feethams, winning ten, drawing twelve and losing only once. We'd also beaten Plymouth twice in the league, so we were hoping it was going to be third time lucky.

I'd only been to Wembley twice previously – the first time to see England play Hungary in November 1981 (Paul Mariner scored the winner in a 1-0 victory), and the second time for the Sherpa Van Trophy Final between Wolves and Burnley in May 1988 (Wolves won the game 2-0 with goals from Andy Mutch and Robbie Dennison). I vowed then that I would never go back unless it was to see Darlington. Well, little did I know that would happen in my lifetime.

To go to Wembley for the first time in the club's 113-year history was a tremendous achievement. Ian organised a coach from Catterick to get us to London. On the way down we saw all sorts of vehicles with black and white scarves and pennants fluttering from their windows, all converging on London, like some modern-day pilgrimage. At motorway service stations mobile teams of hawkers were selling unofficial Darlington merchandise, from rosettes at a pound each to flags on flimsy sticks at a fiver apiece.

On Wembley Way itself all you could see were men in Quaker hats or frizzy black and white wigs and little kids with painted faces, waving about yellow foam rubber hands with pointed index fingers.

The moment the team emerged on to the pitch in the blazing sunshine was something I'll never forget. I'd never seen so many Darlington fans at a game before – there were about 13,000 altogether. Not only that, even though we were outnumbered more than two to one by the Plymouth hordes the 43,431 attendance was a record for a Third Division Play-Off Final. And rather than watching a Cup Final on television here I was watching my team, the team I had supported since I was a boy of seven. 'Are you watching, Hartlepool!' chanted the massed ranks of Darlington fans. It was a moment to savour.

As for the game, it was a case of missed chances. I can vividly recall, for example, Mattie Appleby's shot in the first half going six inches wide of the post. If only. Though I did smile at the sight of a male streaker appearing from the Darlington end with a Darlo scarf around his head and hurdling the advertising boards behind the goal before the stewards bundled him away to safety. But then, in the second half, came the knockout blow when Plymouth's Ronnie Mauge scored with a free header from a corner. And yet, even then, it might not have been all over when Robbie Painter desperately tried to stretch another six inches to reach a Steve Gaughan cross with the goal at his mercy.

The only blot on that day, apart from the result, was the fact that John Gray was beaten up outside the stadium by some Plymouth supporters. That was awful, because John is a quiet, inoffensive lad, and has never been a football hooligan in his life. Although we lost 1-0 I'll never forget the day I went to Wembley with Darlington FC.

Even before our Wembley appearance the team had already started to disintegrate. Mattie Appleby had turned down a new contract and was sold to Barnsley for £200,000 in the summer. Gary Bannister retired. Sean Gregan was sold to Preston North End in February of the following year for £300,000 and Robbie Blake was transferred to Bradford City for £300,000 in March. Once again, it was the same old story of selling the family silver to appease the club's creditors. Would we ever learn?

Chapter 17

Jane didn't go with me to Wembley or to any of the other games that season, but that didn't bother me because I knew she wasn't interested in football. It was obvious, though, that the strong bond that had existed between us had become steadily weaker with the passage of time. Her changed behaviour towards me became even more noticeable after she made a new female friend. Of course, I certainly didn't mind her going out with her friends, if that's what she wanted. Unlike her possessive husband, I didn't try to chain her to the kitchen sink. I always let her have her independence and, on the whole, she did what she pleased.

But now, it had reached the stage that she would say she couldn't see me on Friday night because she was going out with the girls. Naturally, I was a bit peeved, not having seen her during the week, but when the same thing happened on Saturday too it was a bit much to take. I resented it because I didn't think it was fair. It was like having a relationship with myself. And so I was quite unhappy at that particular time and we had numerous heated arguments.

One night on the telephone Jane was horrible to me about my disability and I was shocked that she could speak to me like that. To be honest, I was in tears, I was absolutely devastated, though I'm sure she never meant it and that her outburst was probably borne out of simple frustration. The next day she rang me up and apologised. But it's not easy to forget things like that.

In September 1996 Jane told me that she didn't want to see me any more. We agreed that a week later I would take a day off work and we'd get together for a chat. Little did I know that Jane already had a new boyfriend in tow. While I was hoping to get things sorted out between us Jane had a new man in her bed.

I saw her now and again, and we actually got back together in October for two or three weeks. It was a short-lived reconciliation because she was still seeing her new boyfriend, who wasn't aware of our relationship. Once again she was living a lie by not telling him. Even though Jane had replaced me with another man I was still happy to see her whenever I could. But I now realise that I should have told her to go for good because it wasn't worth all the heartache that was to follow. As usual she promised me the earth, but to me it seemed as if she was playing some sort of sick game with my emotions.

We decided to call it a day in November, but in December she phoned me up to say that she'd had a big argument with her current boyfriend and she was terribly upset. After talking on the phone for hours on end we got back together. Once more she promised to make a fresh start and said that she was sorry. The first few weeks were like when we'd first met – she was hardly away from my side, and I think she did genuinely try to make a success of it. But we were both mistaken if we thought it would last.

Really, she just began doing the same old things all over again. She would go out with her friends, never giving any thought to my wishes, and the only time I ever saw her now was on a Saturday night, if I was lucky. The crunch came in between Christmas and New Year. Jane told me that she didn't want to be with me all the time because she wanted to share herself between me and someone else, which I thought was rather an odd thing to say.

What upset me was that she freely admitted that she didn't particularly like her new boyfriend and was only attracted to him sexually. I still hadn't recovered from my previous suicide attempt and that set me back in a big way. In a moment of weakness I took my third overdose, which I now realise was a stupid thing to do. But I was really down and hadn't been right for four years.

Luckily, my former lodger found me and took me to the hospital. Apart from being ill for a couple of days, I soon recuperated – physically, that is.

Although Jane was quite upset at the time, having realised what her mental games had done to me, she soon resorted to her familiar tactics. She could be so cruel and insensitive in what she said to me. Maybe it was my own fault and maybe I should have walked away in September, but I didn't because I loved her so much. Once the bad times outweigh the good you ought to call it a day. That was the mistake I made.

Over Christmas I felt desperately ill and didn't enjoy the festivities at all. My sister was the only person who understood what I was going through. No one else could. I was in so much pain. I'll never let another woman do that to me again. It felt like being on a rollercoaster ride – you either cling on or you are thrown off. If it hadn't have been for the support of Alison and my friends I don't think I would have been here to tell the tale.

Although Jane and I still continued to see each other into 1997 it was never quite the same. The thing that finally made up my mind that we had no future together, was when she slept with the husband of one of her ex-neighbours on a one-night stand. What really made it unacceptable was that the man's wife was pregnant at the time, though, in mitigation, I should add that she was drunk when it happened. That certainly made me alter my opinion of her. Although she had done things previously of which I didn't approve I'd never quite lost respect for her. Once you lose respect for someone, though, the relationship's over. I'm no angel myself – far from it –

but I always think I've kept my dignity.

When she told me about that infidelity I was shocked. I can also remember a night when we slept together and halfway through our lovemaking she said that it wasn't as good as with her former boyfriend. I was devastated: the insensitive timing of that remark stopped me in my tracks. I don't profess to be a great lover by any means, but no one had ever complained before. To actually treat someone like that was unforgivable.

It made me think back to the time when she had criticised her husband's sexual inadequacies. The wheel had come full circle and now here I was on the receiving end of her withering comments. Once again I remembered how all my friends, including Ian, John and Robbo, had told me I was wasting my time with her.

Even the Valentine's Day card she sent me in February showed one small but subtle change of emphasis. In her previous cards she had written, 'All my love, Jane' but this one simply said, 'Love, Jane.' Two weeks later, a few days before my birthday, we decided to call it a day. I can recall the phone conversation quite vividly. Jane said that she didn't love me any more and that she had met somebody else, but hadn't slept with him yet. However, she did add that if I ever needed her help at any time in the future she would do all she could for me.

So I never did get a decent birthday with her. The first time I was in intensive care, the second time was when we fell out and the third time...she wasn't even there. However, once I'd made up my mind not to see her it was as if a great weight had been lifted from my shoulders, and my health improved immeasurably from then onwards.

For a while, after we broke up in March, she was still renting Steve Tupling's house, but then she moved back to her neighbourhood on the outskirts of Darlington. We finished on a Sunday and on the following Tuesday I actually saw her next boyfriend taking her kids to school, which would indicate that she had been seeing him for some time.

Now, looking back, I spent six months trying to save something that wasn't even worth saving. I can honestly say, though, that I had some of the best moments of my life with Jane. I can never forget the time that we went to a hotel together and made love the whole day. I can remember that we took some old clothes, got dressed up in them and then playfully ripped them off each other. She even tied me up with some strips of the torn fabric.

However, the downside was that her selfish behaviour contributed to at least one of my suicide attempts, and all I'll say now is, what a waste. I don't hold any grudges against Jane because I know I'm much stronger as a result of the experience.

It's frightening to realise the effect another person can have on your life. For a long time she had a stranglehold over me. In fact, I think we both had a hold over each other. But for her to be partly to blame for my suicide attempt and apparently not feel any remorse is unforgivable.

Like any lover I wrote her letters and bought her flowers and chocolates. I was besotted with her. I even put my flat up for sale and we began looking for a suitable bungalow that we could share. Then, over a period of time, she decided that she couldn't handle my disability. I'd already been going out with her for two years when the issue of my disability came up as a potential obstacle. She could make me feel so small and insignificant by saying horrible things to me. She once said that she wanted a 'proper' man, someone who could do the decorating for her and who she could lean on, but I think she was just scared of the commitment.

It took me from March onwards to get over her. But it wasn't as bad this time round because I knew I didn't want to see her any more after hearing of her indiscretion with her neighbour.

I've often wondered why so many men are drawn to her. She certainly is physically attractive to men, and knows how to manipulate them. She also loves sex. But if a woman likes sex she can go to a nightclub and get picked up anytime. It doesn't prove that the man likes her, just that he wants a lay. To my knowledge, though, she only ever picked up one person from a nightclub and that was the incident I've already mentioned.

I occasionally think about her now, but I've never been tempted to phone her. Why should I when I have my memories? If I live to be ninety I'll be sitting on the commode, old and wrinkled, thinking about those memories. I've since learned that she's sorted herself out, has been with the same partner for over a year now and seems to be happy. I can honestly say that I'm pleased about that. Above all, I want this account to be fair. I've written about my relationship with her as it happened. She could be very caring – when I was in hospital she risked everything to be near me, which is something I'll never forget. And although she occasionally lied to her husband, she was generally honest in her dealings with me, even to the extent of admitting her shortcomings. We certainly had some great laughs together, but it's a part of my life that's over now.

Chapter 18

Apart from two one-night stands, for a period of about ten months I lived quite contentedly without a girlfriend. In any case, football still provided a focus to my life, and Darlington had, or so it seemed, a new saviour in the shape of Mike Peden, who took a majority shareholding in the club at the start of the 1997-98 season. His firm, Chaddington Property & Development Co. Ltd, would be responsible for the re-development of Feethams. On the 21st of October a new era in the history of the club was inaugurated, with the demolition of the old East Stand. Optimism was rife amongst the fans.

That evening the talk in the pub was of the demolition and little else. Raffle tickets were selling briskly inside the ground so that people could vie for the right to press the red plunger and set off the explosion. I was a bit concerned at the thought of debris falling on the pitch, but it was obvious that any demolition would be largely symbolic, given the fact that Feethams is a residential area.

When the moment of the detonation arrived, a compere from the local radio station, Alpha 103.2, tried to maximise the impact of the event by whipping up the crowd, counting down the seconds like a Nasa mission controller. There was a loud bang and a row of fireworks along the front of the East Stand spluttered into life and threw out showers of sparks. Then the moment we were all waiting for finally arrived: a crane hoisted a corrugated iron panel from the barrel roof and lifted it clear. That was it! Later, the crane lowered the panel back in position. You feel the word 'anticlimax' was invented for an occasion such as this.

The game itself against Cardiff City proved to be yet another damp squib and petered out in a dreary 0-0 draw. Perhaps the only noteworthy event was that two Austrians, Mario Dörner and Franz Resch, made their full debuts for the Quakers. Anthony Carss – himself a former Quaker – played for the Bluebirds that night and his main contribution was clearing a shot from Glenn Naylor off his goal line.

The following month we were drawn at home against non-league minnows Solihull Boro in the first round of the FA Cup. When we eventually played them on the 15th of November, we were fourth from bottom of the league. So much for the pre-season hype and misplaced optimism. Even though we were pitted against a team from the Dr Martens Midland Division, we played ultra-cautiously with five at the back. Solihull were 1-0 down in less than a minute after Glenn Naylor scored straight from the kick-off, but Nicky Cross equalised with a header in the 60th minute and the Midlanders managed to hold us to a 1-1 draw. Quakers were deservedly booed off the pitch.

On the 26th of November I made the long journey to Hall Green in south Birmingham for the replay. I went with Ian on one of the coaches that Mike Peden had provided free of charge, leaving Park Place at about three in the afternoon. The universal feeling on board the Supporters' Club coach was that Mike Peden was a hero.

It was a very wet day and when we reached Solihull's Moorlands ground, which they shared with Moor Green FC, we found that the away end was uncovered, so I got soaking wet on the terraces, along with the rest of the five hundred or so Darlington contingent.

The game itself was marred by the referee. Uriah Rennie, the official in charge, dished out eight bookings and sent off Quakers' Lee Turnbull on sixty-eight minutes, only just after he'd come on as a substitute, for elbowing the Solihull keeper. Then Mr Rennie remained obstinately deaf to the whistles of the Darlington fans, even though the ninety minutes were well and truly up. Despite playing with ten men, we were leading 3-2, with a penalty from Brian Atkinson and goals from Paul Robinson and Dörner, yet minute after minute went ticking by, with no sign of an end in sight. Solihull eventually got an equaliser *eleven* minutes into injury time and Mr Rennie played a further minute after that just for good measure! With the sides level after thirty minutes of extra time, the match then went into a nerve-jangling penalty shoot-out. This time luck was on our side, and we ran out 4-3 victors, with Jason de Vos, our Canadian international, scoring the decisive penalty kick.

On New Year's Eve, 1998, I was in the Colburn Lodge pub with members of Ian's immediate family when I happened to bump into an old friend called Heather.

You may recall that Heather helped me with my wheelchair push to Hartlepool in 1991. Anyway, when I saw her I went over to her table and asked if I could buy her a drink. She said she was just on the point of leaving with her friend, but gave me her telephone number and suggested I call her. I asked Ian's dad, Dennis, to ring her on my behalf and he invited her back to his house for a small family party. Ironically, before we'd started out that night, I'd said to Dennis, 'Whatever you do, don't let me get fixed up with any women tonight.' He just smiled when I said that.

To my surprise, Heather said she'd come, and when I arrived at the house she was already there.

Later, I got out of my wheelchair and sat on the settee next to Ian's brother, Graeme. During the course of our conversation I mentioned

Heather, asking him, 'Do you reckon I should go for it?' Without hesitation he replied, 'Yes.'

When it was time for her to leave the party, I asked Heather if it would be all right for me to go back to her house. She agreed and pushed me there in my wheelchair – barely a ten-minute walk. Once inside, she opened me a can of lager and we sat on the sofa chatting. Soon, we were all over each other and decided to move on to the bedroom. She dragged me up the stairs one by one, pausing half way up to say, 'This better be worth it, Paul!'

We saw each other for the next six months, but the situation was complicated because Heather had two children. Unlike Jane, when Heather came to visit me she often brought her children with her. We therefore didn't spend much time on our own, and, as I was single, I'm afraid I didn't have a great deal of patience with them. I didn't like the mess they caused. I liked Heather, but not enough to marry her. She talked about making her house more wheelchair-friendly and of me moving in with her. We even had someone from Social Services call with a view to having alterations made.

But things were moving too fast – I know that now. When I first met Jane I felt an adrenaline-rush of excitement, but with Heather I didn't have that same feeling. Heather was quite perceptive about this and said to me one day, 'Paul, I can never be Jane.' I should add, though, that I liked being with Heather. She was good company. I thought I loved her, but looking back now I suppose I didn't love her enough to sacrifice everything.

On the 7th of March 1998, we made the mistake of getting engaged. Before I went ahead with the engagement I had my doubts about the whole affair. There didn't seem to be the same kind of intensity about my relationship with Heather as there had been with Jane. Maybe I did it to prove to myself that I could get another woman.

I booked a pub called the Dalesman for the engagement party. It was a double celebration since it was also my birthday and that of my sister. When we arrived I realised I'd forgotten the ring – surely a bad sign – and Heather had to drive back to my house to retrieve it.

There were about twenty guests in the pub that night, including Steve Tupling and his wife Louise. After the meal Steve pulled me aside and asked me if I was sure about the engagement. He said that it didn't seem right. I didn't look like someone who had just become engaged. My friend Steve Keeney also had grave doubts. I knew by June that I didn't want to marry Heather. Fortunately, she felt the same way. We'd started to get on each other's nerves and argued frequently.

I went away on holiday to Benidorm with Steve Keeney. This time apart from Heather gave me the chance to clear my mind and see the relationship in perspective. By the time I returned, I knew I didn't want to get back with her. She felt the same way. Once I'd decided to split up with her, it was easy to carry it through. Whereas I'd been devastated over the break-up with Jane, this time I recovered fairly quickly. Heather and I are still friends and keep in touch by phone, so at least it ended amicably.

That year was certainly an eventful one. My life seemed to be changing from month to month. In July 1998, for example, I received a telephone call at work to inform me that I'd successfully completed my HNC course in Business and Finance at Darlington College of Technology. This was the culmination of two years of quite intensive study. Once again I was thankful to my employer at the time, Farmway Ltd, for allowing me to continue with my studies and add to the GNVQ in Advanced Business that I'd gained in 1995.

A month later, to complete a noteworthy year, I got myself another job as a Claims Clerk with County Durham TEC. Coincidentally, when I took up my post I found myself working in the very same building in Valley Street, Darlington, where I'd spent my work placement with the Employment Service back in 1989. It was the Employment Service who were now to provide my new employer with a stair-climber, my office being upstairs. Later, I was relocated to Newton Aycliffe.

My last few months at Farmway had been soured by accusations of incompetence. I was told that I was making too many elementary typing errors and that my mind wasn't on my job. My manager informed me that unless things improved I'd be sacked. However, when I went to see an optician a few weeks later I discovered that it had been my failing eyesight to blame for the mistakes, not a lack of concentration on my part.

This isn't the whole story. In the months leading up to this incident I'd already been advised to look for another job. I was told that customers couldn't understand me on the telephone because of my stammer, which totally destroyed my confidence. My job description had also changed. Whoever did my job in the future would be expected to get parts for boilers off the shelves – something which was physically impossible for me to do, so the offer of a new job camc at just the right time for me.

My domestic circumstances also changed at this time. Over a two-year period I'd built up a great rapport with my home carer, Mandy, who worked for County Durham Care. Obviously, when someone is looking after you for five days a week it's only natural that you become close. I thought the world of her. We had a great working relationship, informal yet strictly professional, which suited me fine. I knew how far I could go with her, and that's how it should be. I cannot speak highly enough of her as a carer, because, at times, I can be one of the most arrogant and demanding people imaginable.

Mandy and I certainly had a laugh together. I can remember one morning when she sneaked into the bathroom and threw cold water over me in the shower as a rather drastic remedy for my stinking hangover. But with Mandy there was always a fine line that neither of us crossed, though I must admit that I came perilously close to it on several occasions, by mercilessly winding her up, for which I humbly apologise.

Mandy left me in April 1999 because she had to go into hospital for an operation. Once again I had problems with the management of the Social Services department. Quite simply, they were unable to cope with the fact that I was working overtime, especially at weekends. At one stage, I had six carers in the week that Mandy was in hospital. I also had a strained relationship with the manager of the home care service. After lengthy discussions with my care manager, we decided it would be best for me to change providers.

What incensed me was that I was paying double taxi fares to get to work. The reason for this is that I had to book a lift bus[1] rather than a normal taxi because I couldn't get a carer to my house early enough to help me into the car. The Disability Act states, however, that a disabled person should be cared for when he or she needs care, not when it's convenient for someone else.

I therefore returned to private provision for my home care needs, using the same company I'd employed previously. The situation I found was still far from ideal. One day, for example, my home carer turned up with a hangover, two black eyes and a bandaged wrist. She reeked of alcohol and it was no surprise to me when she admitted that she'd drank a whole bottle of Bacardi the night before. I took a dim view when she vomited it all up in my toilet not long after she arrived. The flat stank horribly afterwards. This was inexcusable and totally unprofessional behaviour.

As far as my general state of health is concerned, I still have my off days. After one particularly severe and prolonged attack of spasms, I had to go to a hospital in Newcastle where I explained to the specialist that I'd flushed my medicines down the toilet. He was naturally horrified by my admission. I still refuse to take medication for my spasms, but my doctor just shakes his

[1]A lift bus is a private-hire vehicle equipped with an electrically-powered hoist at the rear that can be operated by the driver.

head now and says, 'You are either very brave or very foolish, Mr Hodgson.' On another occasion his considered verdict was, 'You have a contempt for life, Mr Hodgson.' I still don't intend to heed his advice, and as for having a contempt for life...

During my consultation with the specialist in Newcastle he explained that it would make sense for me to receive a course of injections in my right leg to stop the damaged muscle going into spasm. The substance they use in this treatment is actually botulinum, the same bacterium that is responsible for food-poisoning! As with all medical procedures, there are certain risks involved. There's a slim chance that I'll be left with no movement in my leg for some time. However, if successful, the injections will prolong my life. Without them I would be at increased risk of suffering a massive and potentially fatal heart attack as the spasms increase in their intensity. After considering all the evidence, for and against, I've decided to go ahead with the treatment.

Also in 1999 I bought myself a better computer, had a modem installed and got connected to the Internet. Here I can read the latest news about Darlington FC, and am able to chat to people on an equal footing as never before. People can't hear my stammer in cyberspace! I also bought myself a track ball to replace the mouse, because that was difficult to operate with my shaky coordination. So you see I'm making the most of modern technology to assist me in my search for even greater independence.

As the reader will have gleaned during the course of this book, Darlington Football Club has been a constant source of stability in my life, through good times and bad. Long may that continue. I still go to as many games as I can, details of which can be read about in a future book.

Despite five years having passed since my mother's death, I still have no contact with my stepsisters, a situation that suits me fine. Apparently, they continue to blame me for my mother's death, which I think is a pitiful state of affairs. I'll leave the reader to reach his or her own conclusions on that subject.

You may also recall that my late mother once told me that I should learn to be as independent as possible. Now that I have a good job and a similar lifestyle to that of any able-bodied person, I feel that I have lived up to her expectations. I sincerely hope that she would be proud of me and my achievements in life so far.